Old at Age 3

The Story of Zachary Moore

**Written By
Keith Moore**

BOSS
publishing

Copyright © 2007, Boss Publishing

For more information on bulk sales, contact:

Boss Publishing, Inc.
601 S. Washington, #119
Stillwater, OK 74074
Or visit us at www.bosspublishing.com

Art and Design: Shane Lansdown

ISBN: 978-0-615-16062-7

Library of Congress Control Number: 2007904211

Printed in the United States of America

Table of Contents

◆ ◆ ◆

Preface

◆ ◆ ◆

Our son's full name is Zachary Kale Moore. We called him Zachary, Zach, ZK, and his favorite and the most appropriate, Boss. I started calling him "Boss" when he was about a year old. I was amazed at his ability to control his life and what went on around him. It felt so natural the first time I called him Boss. He seemed so pleased to be called the Boss, and it quickly became his preferred nickname. Anyone who knew him agreed Boss was an appropriate nickname, and nobody ever disputed his claim to this title. We primarily called him Boss or Zachary, depending on the conversation.

How great it was to be bossed by Zachary! Boss had everyone's best interest in mind, and had more confidence than anyone I knew. Once Boss had made a decision around our house, it was final. Even more amazing was his ability to make the right decision. Boss never let our family down or led us astray. When we were together, he knew what I was going to do before I did. I often found myself asking Boss for advice. He always knew the best choices that my adult heart and mind were afraid or hesitant to make. I guess this was because of his pure and honest intentions. When I walked him he would direct me by leaning or pointing and provide me with necessary corrections by barking his commands and raising his hand to point. I respected how he controlled without throwing fits like a normal child might have. He truly had the qualities a successful boss should have.

I don't know if Zachary was chosen by God to live a life filled with challenges. I do know Zachary overcame his ultimate challenges by living a righteous life within his short lifespan. I also believe all of us are faced with our own challenges and we too have the power through faith in God for our own personal victory. I am sorry that I can't write a story about how Zachary eventually physically overcame life's challenges, but I am proud to present his story of miraculous works for the time he was here. One thing that Zachary has taught everyone: Your Attitude, Your Choice!

Foreword by Chip Foose

◆ ◆ ◆

There are those that are born with an unfair condition that will rob them of their lives long before they should leave this earth. We see these cases in our everyday lives—on the news, in magazines, and even in our own cities, towns, and homes. And some of them shine so brightly that we cannot feel pity; rather only happiness at knowing them and the hope that they may someday be cured. These individuals serve as role models, offer joy to all who meet them, provide the most precious of friendships, and have a zest for life unequalled by anyone else I've known. They are the truest example of hope and inspiration.

My name is Chip Foose. I am a car designer and host of TLC's 'Overhaulin', and I've had the pleasure of knowing more than one of these heroes. My sister Amy died in 1985 from Progeria at age sixteen from a heart attack. The disease has had a profound impact on my life, from the constant dedication my family had towards Amy every day of her life, to my later becoming deeply involved with The Progeria Research Foundation. But it was through my sister, Jodi, that I first met Zachary Moore.

Jodi had known Zachary for 5 months and had told my wife Lynn and I many stories about the new little love in her life. After our mother calmed Jodi's many apprehensions of resurfacing pain about losing Amy, she first met Zach at his third birthday party, a fundraiser called *Hunting for a Cure* because of Zach's love of hunting. In Zach's routine nature, he immediately opened a door in her heart that she had shut years ago. From his happy little voice and giggly nature to his cute mannerisms, Jodi fell in love with her new little friend. She found herself spending many of her days at the Moore home in Stillwater, playing with Zach and forming a very close bond to the Moore family. Jodi introduced me to Keith, Molly, and Zachary Moore in November 2005. I was accepting *The Amy Award* from The Progeria Research Foundation in Boston, and Zach was there with his parents. I was amazed at how tiny he was and loved the way he lit up when he saw my sister and yelled "Jodi!" in his happy little tone, excited as always to see his dear friend. I spent that evening drawing race cars and cartoons with Zach and, for the first time, I fully understood what past friends had meant when they said they fell in love with Amy after just a short time of getting to know her, for this was how I felt about Zach. He continually made you smile, even when faced with a seemingly disastrous disability.

I can now say that it was not a job but an honor to be brought up in a household where my parents fought so hard for so many years for my sister, treating her as any other child and making sure she had the same opportunities as her peers and siblings. It has been an equal honor to support The Progeria Research Foundation, and it fills me with pride to have been a part of Zach's life and now a part of this remarkable story of inspiration. God bless all of those with Progeria, and God bless their families. Together we *WILL* find a cure!

—Chip Foose

Part I

Introduction

◆ ◆ ◆

Molly and I had been married five months and we lived in Stillwater, Oklahoma. With this marriage, in addition to a great wife, I gained three wonderful stepchildren, Derek, Courtney, and Lindsay, aged five, six, and ten respectively. Not only was this marriage new to me, but so was parenting for I had no children until now. Becoming an instant parent of three kids was challenging for me, not to mention that Molly was pregnant with what would be my first biological child. Everything was new, and I was doing my best to gain control of our situation.

Molly, Courtney, and Derek moved to the town where I was living, and Lindsay stayed with her biological father in her hometown. It was only a couple of hours in distance, but it was still a change for them all. Things were going smoothly and as planned for our family. We were living in a small two-bedroom farmhouse rental, but we were building a new home located in a quiet neighborhood that would be all we needed and wanted for our family.

Yes, I was a new husband, a new father, and a new home-owner. I thought my life was hectic and rather demanding, but we were making it through it all. But this is not a story about me—it's a story about Zachary—and what happens next changed the lives of many people for the best!

When Molly was seven months pregnant, we were starting to have thoughts about getting ready for the baby's arrival, planning details of the birth, and coordinating a brief hospital stay, because that's what you do when you have a healthy baby. The kids were excited about having a new addition to the family, and we had signed them up for a sibling class at the hospital. We had been debating for months on names, and some of the names that the kids suggested sounded more like names for a pet. Molly and I kept busy with work and designing the new home we were building so it would be a perfect environment for our family. We were living the life we wanted, and everything ahead of us seemed so certain and promising.

It was the long and relaxing weekend of the Fourth of July holiday when late one evening after watching an ice cream commercial we decided to take a drive to town to a local ice cream store for a treat. Wearing flip-flops on our feet and with only a few dollars in the pockets of our shorts, we left the house thinking we would be right back. A few miles from the house, Molly announced, much to my shock, that she thought her water had just broken. My understanding, based on the pregnancies portrayed on every movie I had seen, was this couldn't be happening now, because this was supposed to happen in the ninth month of a pregnancy! She immediately assured me that it was indeed happening right then, eight weeks earlier than planned. All I could say was, "Does this mean we are not going to have ice cream?" She hastily informed me I needed to forget about the ice cream and proceed to the hospital.

Instantly I understood the seriousness of this moment, as if someone had just enlightened me to the knowledge that I was in fact not in control in spite of all our planning and knowledge of the way things should be. I can vividly remember today the spot on the road to the hospital and my prayer to God as I sped ahead on our new journey. Molly apologized for certainly damaging the leather seat in my truck from her water breaking on it. I let her know that I was not too worried about my truck seat at this time. When we arrived at the emergency room, Molly did not want to get out of the truck, since it appeared she had wet her pants. What a time to worry about appearances! I assured her that she looked very pregnant and that they would understand. Rather than getting into a prolonged dispute about her wet pants I made due. I handed her one of my work shirts from the back seat and she wrapped it around her waist.

I had limited knowledge of the medical capabilities for premature births and so I figured our pregnancy was over and our child was lost. I did not know that premature births are fairly common and often successful. Sensing the seriousness of our situation, I feared the worst for our child, and I knew I could only turn to God and ask for strength and his blessings on our family. **I prayed God would give me this child and I would always love him and provide for him with all my might no matter the circumstances. This was the first of many prayers about my son that God would answer.**

The local hospital did not have the capabilities for such a premature birth, so Molly was rushed by ambulance to Saint Francis Hospital in Tulsa, where they had a state of the art facility to care for premature births. When the ambulance left the hospital, I headed back home to grab a few things. My mind was racing with what was happening in that ambulance. Molly told me later that the paramedics just kept telling her not to have that baby in their ambulance! I was able to call our family to let them know the situation and they were at the hospital when she arrived. When I got to the hospital, I was relieved to see that my son had not been born yet. The doctors told us that it would be best if we could hold labor off for a few days and administer steroids to try and mature the baby's lungs. After four days of labor filled with uncertainty, pain, and prayer, Molly gave birth to our son on July 7, 2002. I was so proud of Molly making it through this difficult labor. Our priorities changed in just a few short minutes. The medical team had warned me about how babies born prematurely often do not have the appearance of full term babies. They informed me he would be rushed away to intensive care and likely be hooked up to various medical devices and placed in a controlled environment.

I prepared myself for the worst, but instead I somewhat calmly watched the birth of my beautiful son. He weighed 3 pounds 14 ounces and looked like most premature babies. I guessed his weight within an ounce. Now that we had Zachary, I felt I understood the task ahead of us, the task of getting our son through this period of complications associated with premature birth so he could become a healthy child. Little did I know or want to suspect that the near future would bring Zachary and us incredible and extremely rare health challenges. Even more unimaginable would be the lessons this physically troubled and small baby would teach us.

I am no stranger to adventures. I have navigated small boats across the ocean in Alaska and held on as the large seas threatened to sink my boat into the cold waters. I climbed the tallest mountain in the world if you consider the mountain's sea floor base, only to become stranded at the top thanks to altitude sickness and lack of gear. That night I almost froze to death in Hawaii, of all places. I have walked the Alaskan bush hunting huge bears with a bow and arrow. With all of these so-called adventures behind me, here I was, looking at my newborn son. As Zachary struggled to take his first breath immediately after birth, I reached down and shook him myself and blew in his face to encourage the first breath, which he then immediately took. **As I write this I think what a real adventure it is for a parent to be there for their child's first breath and last breath. This is the story of my adventures with Zachary between those two breaths.**

The Journey

◆ ◆ ◆

Our baby was lying in a crib in the hospital intensive care unit as I stood over him and gave thanks to God for him. I pondered what to name him and finally decided on Zachary Kale Moore. Molly was exhausted after four days of labor and having a c-section so the doctors gave her some medicine so she would rest. When she awoke she immediately asked about the baby. I told her God was taking care of him. She asked what we were going to name him. We had compiled a list of a few names we had all agreed upon. I asked what she thought about the name Zachary Kale Moore, which was not one of the names on the list, and she said she liked it. I told her that was good because that is what I had named him while she was sleeping! The kids had been visiting family over the holiday. They had just arrived and were now trying to look at their new brother through the glass window into the Neonatal Intensive Care Unit, or EOPC. Because of the strict visitation guidelines for the unit, that was as close as they could get. Molly tried explaining what had happened and that their brother was going to need special care at the hospital for a while before he could come home. The unit was very large, and all they could see was the crib where he was laying. Molly explained that he had some tubes and monitors hooked up to him so they wouldn't be too frightened. One of the nurses could see them with their noses pressed firmly against the window, trying to get a glimpse of the brother they had excitedly been waiting for. She picked up Zachary and held him so they could get a look at their new brother. I remember them saying that he was so small that he looked like a doll, but he was the cutest thing they had ever seen.

At the time we had no idea he had any health problems beyond being born eight weeks prematurely. We hoped he would only require special care until he could catch back up with the health of a full-term baby. Molly and I were healthy parents. We were both in great physical condition and practiced healthy living habits. All our other children had normal health and we had no previous experience with severe health conditions.

Over the next few weeks I bounced back and forth daily between the hospital, our other children, and work. Molly moved into the nearby Ronald McDonald House so she could stay with Zachary. She spent the entire six weeks caring for Zachary in the hospital until he was healthy enough for us to take him home. Molly dedicated her life to our son and only left the hospital to sleep. She was at Zachary's side throughout his time there. During this period we intensely cared for Zachary, and we hoped and even assumed we would get him through his struggle with premature birth and to a point of normal health.

The kids and I would make the 1½ hour drive several times a week to see Zachary and Molly. She would tell the kids how much she missed and loved them, but right now Zachary needed her there to take care of him and when he was able to come home, she would really need their help. They would bring pictures they had colored for their brother and the nurses would hang them near his crib. We had family that lived in the area and they would come up during visitation hours when we could open the curtains into the unit so they could see Zachary. For the first couple of weeks, Molly and I were only allowed to hold him during feedings, which were about every two hours and only lasted a few short minutes. Those few minutes were some of the happiest in my life. Zachary continued to get stronger and we were so thankful our prayers were being answered. We continued to pray for our son and also for all the other babies and families in the hospital facing similar situations. We developed friendships with other parents and rejoiced with them when they received good news about their babies and cried with them when the news wasn't so good. All the babies had signs on their cribs with their names. Sometimes when our kids would visit, they would notice some of the signs were different and would ask where the other babies went. We would just tell them that they got to go home. We didn't say that sometimes "home" meant with their families and sometimes "home" meant heaven.

And then I got the call. Molly called to let me know they thought Zachary would get to come home the next day. He would have to be sent home on a heart and respiratory monitor and several medications. The hospital staff would train us what to do if the monitor's alarm sounded. What a joyous day it was when we left the hospital and started home with our baby! We telephoned home to let the kids know we were on our way. They were squealing with excitement, with the news of our much-awaited arrival. Courtney asked where we were and how much longer until we were home. I explained to her that we had just passed a point in the road known as the Stillwater Y and were crossing the bridge that was right after that. She immediately declared the spot "Zachary's Bridge." Even today when we cross this bridge, she will mention this is where we were when we called and said he was coming home. She still calls it Zachary's Bridge.

We were so proud of him and hoped that all his health problems would soon be behind him. It seemed just about the time he was starting to show signs of overcoming his premature birth that new problems began to arise. Just when we thought we were nearing good health for Zachary, a new set of concerns developed. After four weeks of being home with Zachary we began to notice changes in him. Over a period of about four more weeks the changes were drastic and Zachary's appearance began to alter from that of a typical baby.

We never could overcome issues with lack of weight gain and started to notice other conditions developing with our son. Over about a two-week period his skin became tight and seemed to not be growing. This tight skin restricted him and presented many other problems. We knew something bigger was wrong with him other than being born prematurely. Zachary was two months old and we now knew he was facing serious and potentially long-term health issues. The reality set in that normal health might no longer be ahead for Zachary. We began extensive medical testing and research of our own to determine what was wrong with our son. Over the next several months we consulted with more than fifty doctors. At one point at a doctor's office, a doctor walked into the room, looked at Zachary briefly and asked if we were Christians. We responded "yes," and she just said we should take him home and pray for him, because he wasn't going to live much longer. We just sat in shock looking at her as she left the room. The process of extensive testing and doctor's visits with no definitive answers was extremely frustrating. The information and technology was just not there for Zachary.

As we visited the medical specialists at various hospitals, there were no definite answers to Zachary's problems. Finally, we were checked into a children's hospital and they suggested that he had Restrictive Dermopathy, a disease that is typically fatal at birth or within a few weeks of it. The doctors let us know to expect the worst soon. They gave him a life expectancy of one to four more weeks. I read the clinical description of the disease and could agree with the doctors that this was in fact a strong possibility and understood why they thought he might have only a few more weeks to live. However, I refused to accept a diagnosis based on a clinical description that had no scientific diagnostic test. I still had hope and knew the possibility of another diagnosis might still be out there, and maybe it would be one that was curable. As long as there remained possibilities, Molly and I would never give up. Therefore, we kept up the search for answers to Zachary's condition.

A few days went by, and Zachary continued to survive. Then another series of potential diagnoses were suggested through the process of elimination. Again, I understood that while the other diagnoses were possible, the exact disease or condition was still not definitive. This meant we did not know how to care for Zachary's condition since we did not necessarily know what the problem was. We would not accept a "likely" diagnosis for our son for fear of later finding out a diagnosis for him that would have been treatable all along. For this reason we kept searching for a definite diagnosis so we could then focus on curing the problem.

Zachary's condition due to his tight skin was alarming at this point. It was affecting his growth, his movement, and, most importantly, his ability to breathe. The sheer tightness of the skin over his torso constricted his lungs. Fortunately his heart was not constricted as well. Zachary was so vulnerable at this point. God answered our prayers to see him through this, and we were able to care for him at home through this difficult three months. Inside Zachary's body was a spirit that would not be denied. He certainly did not know of any other existence than the one he was given. Therefore, he strived to develop in whatever way his body would allow. Even more amazing was his happiness throughout all of the health difficulties.

The frustration of not knowing what was wrong with our son took hold of Molly and me. The only thing we knew for sure was that Zachary had something seriously wrong with him. We hoped for a diagnosis of a disease we would be able to fix. At this point, even a terminal diagnosis would seem like a victory for us. At least with that, we would know what to expect and how to care for Zachary. All Molly and I could do was pray, care for Zachary the best we knew how, and keep searching for an accurate diagnosis. So we took care of Zachary at home and did just that.

We experienced different levels of care with each hospital or doctor we visited. We would go through an exam or testing with a particular doctor who claimed he could diagnose Zachary. Then we would go home, and days would go by and we would not receive any word of follow up from the doctor or the doctor's office. No test results, conclusions, or even suggestions. The only follow-up communication we would get would be an invoice in the mail asking for payment of services. Their idea of service and my idea of service were obviously different. Mine involved some kind of a result provided. I would have been satisfied with a follow-up phone call informing me that they had reviewed the exam and test results performed on my son and they had no idea what was wrong with him. This would have been the professional thing to do. I suspect these particular doctors' egos would not permit them to do such a thing. Instead, we would finally write letters requesting the test results for our medical file in hopes they would be beneficial later on as we continued on with our research.

In contrast to this poor treatment, we also worked with doctors and hospitals that were a tremendous help in caring for Zachary. We visited hospitals funded by charitable organizations and they really tried to help Zachary. During these visits we were able to see the good work these hospitals were doing for sick children.

Zachary's personal physician and staff were very accommodating to him. They all knew him since he was in their facility often. It seemed they gave him preferential treatment because they were well aware of his challenges. We could hear the nurses out in the hallway arguing because nobody wanted the duty of giving him a shot or making him cry. The nurses wanted to stay in favor with Zachary and giving him a shot was not the way to win him over. They drew straws to see who would give the shot. They all worked so hard to make things easy on him. Zachary's physician made herself so accessible to us that we were even able to call her on her mobile phone during her vacation. This doctor developed quite a relationship with Zachary and it was obvious she deeply cared for him as a person as much as she cared for him as a patient.

Because Zachary was born prematurely, he was eligible for a free program through the state called Sooner Start. It is for children between the ages of newborn to three years with developmental delays to help them catch up with other children their ages. John Jennings, an occupational therapist, visited our home every Thursday at 10:00 A.M. for three years! He was also a great resource for questions that we had. He would suggest exercises to try and keep Zachary as flexible as possible, and ideas on how to get more calories in his food to help battle the issue of Zachary not gaining weight. Through this program, Molly was able to learn how to provide physical therapy for Zachary. The weekly visits were used to determine the therapy Zachary would receive throughout the week. Molly would then provide the physical therapy to Zachary five times each day. This consisted of stretching, exercise, and massage.

Molly and I did extensive research on our own. We used resources such as books, the Internet, and doctors across the county. If an in-person visit was not practical due to geography, we would simply email photographs of Zachary with a list of physical symptoms and test results already performed, and conduct a teleconference with the medical professional. Molly started a medical journal containing all of Zachary's medical information for quick reference. Sometimes doctors would suggest a certain test be done and we could check to see if it had already been completed and what the results were. We didn't want Zachary to go through more traumatic testing if it wasn't necessary. It also contained notes from hospital visits, physicians' records, medication he was taking, and even photos to show new doctors the progression of his disease. This medical journal proved very useful and saved us much time and effort in caring for Zachary. As we traveled from medical center to medical center and health issue to health issue, having a central file of all Zachary's medical information that we could take with us was a great idea.

Through our research my eyes were opened to the many health problems a child can have. There were hundreds of diseases I had never imagined were out there. I began to understand the actual percentages of unhealthy children. I gained an even greater appreciation of good health and an expanded compassion for children who were sick. There are many health problems that can occur with a child. A healthy child truly is a miracle and not something a parent should take for granted.

At the age of six months Zachary's mental development was very normal and quite impressive. However, his physical appearance took on drastic changes as he began to lose his hair and his skin remained extremely tight, so much so it was like the tightness of the leather over a football. This resulted in contractures of most of his major joints. His head began to grow larger than his body and his face. These are all symptoms of a condition known as progeria. Some doctors picked up on this and began to suggest Zachary may have progeria.

Molly and I read the description of this disease. It is a rare, fatal, genetic condition characterized by an appearance of accelerated aging in children. Most children with progeria are born looking healthy and then show characteristics of the condition around the age of two. Hutchinson-Gilford Progeria Syndrome (HGPS) is the typical progeria and affects 1 child in 4 million to 8 million births. Compare this to studies that suggest your odds of getting struck by lightning are 1 in 600,000. Progeria results in death at an average age of 13 years. The children die of heart disease, heart attacks, or stroke and experience many other conditions normally associated with elderly people, like arthritis and osteoporosis.

This was the most likely diagnosis for Zachary, but again, without a scientific test, an actual diagnosis was not possible. This was extremely frustrating, because we did not know how to plan, care, or focus our efforts. A clinical or scientific diagnosis could not be made because Zachary's symptoms did not match that of typical progeria and there was no screening test at that time. And he had developed the condition much earlier than the typical age of two.

We discovered The Progeria Research Foundation, which is a non-profit organization dedicated to developing treatments and a cure for progeria through research and education. The Progeria Research Foundation was created to raise awareness, to educate and help the families, their doctors, researchers and the general public about progeria, and to find a cure. The foundation was formed in 1999 by the family of Sam Berns, a child with progeria.

In 2003, The Progeria Research Foundation helped discover the gene for HGPS and was then able to develop a diagnostic test for it. The test was given on Zachary's cell line and they were able to determine he probably had a form of progeria but not the typical HGPS. This was all made possible through the work of The

Progeria Research Foundation. Even though the results of this scientific test confirmed that Zachary had a terminal disease, we received much comfort in finally knowing for sure what our son's health problem was. It is hard to imagine that anyone could find any comfort in knowing his child had a terminal illness. However, there were actually many good things about this diagnosis in spite of the obvious over riding factor that it was terminal.

With the news of the terminal diagnosis, there was not much of an initial shock. By this point we knew something serious was wrong with our child. At least now we finally knew for sure that there was not something Molly and I were or were not doing that was right or wrong for him. We were able to make decisions about having another child since this condition was not hereditary. As bad as the news was for us, it still gave us peace knowing we did not need to keep looking for an answer. Instead we could focus on providing day-to-day care and finding a treatment or cure for progeria. To be able to focus our efforts on the actual problem was an achievement. So we somehow managed to view the news of a terminal diagnosis as good news.

Immediately our focus shifted from trying to get an accurate diagnosis to finding a cure for our son's condition. We were very involved with numerous doctors and research teams trying to figure out how to care or perhaps treat Zachary's condition. Unfortunately we could only provide care for his symptoms and not his overall condition. Zachary never received any form of treatment for progeria. None was available, and work had only been going on a short while to find a cure. Still we never gave up hope. Zachary was always our priority and we were optimistic about his condition. We hoped and believed we would find a cure, but we treated Zachary like there was no tomorrow.

I involved myself at the technical level of progeria research. I provided patient-specific information and consulted with scientists performing the research. I communicated often with the leading research scientists, and I was diligent in providing input from the patient representative perspective. This would range from technical answers to words of encouragement and appreciation. I felt it was important to let the scientists know how thankful we were for the work they were doing and the progress they were making.

Later in his life Zachary participated in a research project led by Dr. Jeffrey Miner at Washington University. The research determined Zachary had a form of progeria much more severe than the typical progeria, which explained why he had exhibited symptoms much earlier in life than was usual. The research indicated Zachary had more of the harmful Lamin A mutations than the typical progeria case. This meant not only did Zachary have a terminal genetic disease, he had a form of it that was the worst ever documented. His form of progeria would lead to more severe symptoms and an even shorter life span than the typical cases.

We raised Zachary with a focus on giving him the love and fun all children deserve. This went on while behind the scenes Molly and I worked exhaustively trying to figure out how to provide medical care to improve Zachary's quality of life. We worked very hard on nutrition issues. Zachary's failure to grow and tight skin presented problems with adequate intake to obtain needed nutrition. We mixed customized drinks and fed him hourly all his life. He required frequent feeding because his stomach was so tight and constricted, allowing only small portions of food intake. The frequent feeding went on day and night. Zachary never slept for more than two hours at a time. At night he would wake up every couple hours and we would change his diaper, feed him, walk him for a while and then go back to sleep. Again we would repeat the process in two hours. These activities went on each night and Molly and I relied on each other to trade off on such duties.

We certainly had our share of sleepless nights, but we did not complain. Instead we kept on with whatever it took each night and each day. We dwelled on the good and enjoyed our moments with Zachary. I walked miles inside our house with Zachary in my arms, sometimes so tired I was sleepwalking and actually deflected off the walls as I walked him during the night when he could not sleep. Surely I could keep my effort up if Zachary could keep going despite all his pain. Zachary was all the motivation Molly and I needed to keep going. We made it through all these nights by praying for strength from God to keep going. We did not question or show anger about our situation. Thankfully I was further along in my walk with God so I could keep walking with Zachary.

Molly and I did not enter into defeatism over our child's illness. Instead we focused on making him happy; allowing the circumstances to unite our entire family, and asking ourselves what good work can we do through this situation to please God. *Oh, it would have been easy for us to become depressed, turn on each other, and even to turn our back on God in anger. Instead we rejoiced in the gift of our son, leaned on each other for support, and turned to God and asked for strength and knowledge to make it through our challenges. I never lost sight of my original answered prayer to God asking Him to give me a son to love.*

We were always busy caring for Zachary. Molly gave him physical therapy five times each day to assist in his development and prevent his contractures from becoming too extreme. We applied lotions hourly to his skin, which was very tight and presented him with much discomfort. Zachary enjoyed the massage part of this process—and who wouldn't? He would direct us on where and how to massage. He was very set in his ways and always let us know how he wanted things done. He would shout out which body part needed to be massaged. His favorite was his back. And we had to give an equal amount of time to each leg or else he would let us know.

Through Zachary's first year-and-a-half of life, he taught and inspired his immediate family by overcoming his challenges, and more importantly, by overcoming these challenges with a righteous attitude. As Zachary's ability to communicate and interact with the world grew, so did this attitude. I watched as Zachary began to impact others, and I began to witness and understand the gift he was to us. My eyes were opened and my heart was softened. I began to consider myself subordinate to Zachary, and my relationship with Zachary was not a normal father-son relationship. But we all know there was nothing normal about Zachary.

After all, Zachary had all these health problems and was given little chance of survival past one month of age, then six months, then ten months. But he kept surviving and was the happiest person I knew! Was this happiness and survival a coincidence, was he truly an angel, did he have some Godly work to do before he would leave, or was this simply the harsh reality of nature taking its course? I still don't know for sure. In reflection I truly believe it was all of these working together.

Having progeria meant Zachary exhibited symptoms that included:

- failure to grow;
- tight skin;
- poor bone density and other skeletal defects;
- a disproportionately small face in comparison to the head;
- prominent veins on the scalp;
- small nose;
- heart disease;
- severe contractures (limited joint movement);
- open fontanels (an open space or soft spot within the skull bone like that observed with typical infants);
- a small airway;
- loss of hair.

Although Zachary's symptoms were severe and life-threatening, it was easy for Molly and I not to see them. Instead we could see his desire to live, need to please others, ability to have fun, and refusal to complain about his situation. These qualities were such a contrast to his actual health, which allowed him to only gain one pound over a six month period. At the age of two he weighed only nine pounds, which was less than half the normal weight of a child his age. He was unable to crawl or walk. He was able to sit up and did learn to scoot across the floor in that posture. Zachary completely lost his hair by the time he was two years old.

Dr. Leslie Gordon at The Progeria Research Foundation informed us that some of the children were having some success with growth issues and failure to thrive by using human growth hormone injections. She let us know that this medication was very costly and took a dedicated commitment. We would have to give Zachary an injection once daily probably for an extended amount of time. After praying about it and discussing it over with several specialists, we decided to move forward. After some haggling with the insurance company, they approved the medication but our cost was still going to be astronomical, about $17,000 a year of which only about $5,000 would be covered by insurance. But what price is too high for possibly helping your child? We gave him daily injections of the human growth hormone.

I was Zachary's preferred means of mobility. He would sit in the palm of my hand facing forward, and I would walk him around while he leaned back on my chest. If he was anxious or in a hurry he would lean forward and direct me by leaning. If he wanted the sensation of walking, I would walk on my knees behind him, and he would balance sitting on my hand and walk using his legs. He would place some of his weight on his legs until he became tired, and then he would rely on my arm to carry him. Needless to say, my knees took much abuse, and I wore out the knees in many pants from walking through the house or the yard together. I could never complain, though; after all if he could keep going surely I could too. At first appearance, it looked as if I could drop Zachary by these methods of getting him around. But he had incredible balance, and we had such a strong mental connection that it was not much different balancing Zachary sitting in my hand than it was to balance my own head sitting on top of my neck. It was practically involuntary. Zachary spent an incredibly high percentage of his time in my arms, and the resulting bond between us meant everything to me. We became very in-tune with each other, and the communication as we walked together seemed effortless. It was very important to me that Zachary felt as if he was walking or moving around by his own power and without my assistance. This was critical in his mental development. A child's ability to explore and move by his own sense of power is often helpful in mental development. This is why I became such an advocate of mobility devices such as wheelchairs. A child receiving mobility is not just a matter of their being able to get from point to point. It is much more than that, especially during this developmental stage of life.

For the most part, we spoiled Zachary, and thankfully he did not become a brat as a result. Instead he just used the attention and opportunities to excel in life. We usually did whatever Zachary wanted to do, and this worked out well because all he ever wanted was to have fun with his family and friends. He was always so eager to please others and a joy for everyone to be around. Zachary's worries were not of his health. Instead he worried about where his brother and sisters were at all times. He worried about when I would get home from work or when Molly would come home from the store. He worried about getting to spend the weekend with his grandparents. He anticipated an approaching party, holiday, or day at school.

Due to his small size and bald head he had the general appearance of a baby rather than a toddler at the age of two. When we would go to eat at a restaurant Zachary would often sit on top of the table and eat from a plate of food. He would be eating the same things adults eat and the looks he got were priceless. One time at a Mexican restaurant a lady actually followed Molly into the restroom and scolded her for feeding a baby spicy guacamole. Molly informed her that 'the baby" was two years old, so the lady stopped her ranting and asked "Well, then, what's wrong with him?' Molly just told her that whatever it was, it wasn't near as bad as what was wrong with her!

People were often confused and at times would even approach our table and say things like, "I've never seen a baby sit up like that and eat a cheeseburger!" They were even more surprised when Zachary would speak to them or ask me for some ketchup. People would often approach us when we were in public and say, "Oh, look at the baby!" For Zachary's benefit, I would correct them and let them know that he was not a baby, but was two years old. At that point the person would kind of look at me and then wander off confused. The most frustrating occurrence is when someone would ask, "What is wrong with your baby?" What do you say to that? I normally explained that he had a rare genetic disorder and thanked them for their concern. Sometimes that was responded to with a "that is so sad," "is there a cure," "how old is he," or even "is he going to die?" Zachary would hear all these conversations and he understood everything. After a while I started using the response, "he has a rare genetic disorder, but his hearing is perfect and he understands everything you say." This was the kindest way I knew to counteract their unintentionally inappropriate questions. It wasn't that we were hiding these things from Zachary, but we did try to ensure he got the respect he deserved.

At the age of three, Zachary weighed 11 pounds and measured 30 inches in height. Zachary was very smart and by that age he successfully tested at a five to six year old level. He could fully communicate, although his diminished lung capacity led his speech to occur in the shortest sentences possible. He often used one word in place of the normal few words. He did, however, have much volume in his voice when needed! He would never back down to a yelling contest with his siblings. Zachary was always active and loved to be on the go. He went everywhere with me and was included in virtually all my activities. There were so few things in my life that Zachary was not involved in. I was blessed in the quality and quantity of time I spent with him.

Zachary's mental development was substantial by the age of three. He understood every concept Molly and I taught him. He was able to read single words, identify colors, count, and operate a computer to play games or open and close files of photographs. He did this by operating the computer mouse. He did not let his physical limitations keep him from doing things. He was very adept at bossing me and others around so we would carry him or use other means for him to get around. Additionally, he scooted around for short distances on his bottom. He wore out several pairs of pants that way. He began operating a small power wheelchair at the age of two and became quite efficient at the joystick style control within hours of beginning use.

Those around Zachary who were struggling themselves often found inspiration in him. We received a letter from a man who said he was down on his luck and extremely depressed. The man explained how he had rented a motel room and planned to commit suicide that evening. He was sitting on the bed with a bottle of liquor in his hand so he could get drunk enough to kill himself. The television set was on and he saw a story on the evening news about Zachary. The story was about Zachary and how he was so happy even with his current challenges and a terminal illness. The story showcased how Zachary was getting a service dog and showed video of Zachary playing and being himself. *The man went on to explain in his letter that after watching Zachary courageously face his problems and find such happiness in life, surely his problems could be overcome, too!* He walked out of the motel room and turned to God.

This is a powerful message on how we can help our fellow man just by the simple act of living an example for others to see. I was so proud of my two-year-old son and the courage of this man in sharing his story with us. By this man simply taking the time and humbly sharing his story with Molly and me, he was in turn able to help us. This man's story inspired Molly and me to continue to face and overcome our own challenges. All of these magnificent occurrences happened, and we never even met in person. *By simply living righteously, we have such power to help each other.*

Molly and I had been reluctant about putting Zachary on the evening news. We had been concerned that he might become a spectacle, and that it could cause our family negative attention. We prayed about it and decided to do the story because the news station promised to use the story to raise money for Southwest Service Dogs, the organization providing Zachary with his service dog. We were fortunate because the news station did have Zachary's best interest in mind. The news story was a wonderful inspirational segment, rather than a sob story to simply capture the public's attention long enough to keep them watching through the commercial break.

After the success of the first story, we agreed to do a series of stories with the news station and Kirsten McIntyre, the news reporter. All of the stories were done in the interest of informing the public about progeria, The Progeria Research Foundation, Southwest Service Dogs, and Zachary's inspiring life. Had we not prayed about this, we likely would never have agreed to do the stories. We did turn down many other opportunities for television interviews because we did not believe or approve in what a program stood for or promoted.

We were fortunate Kirsten found us and did such a great job with the series of stories on Zachary. We have received hundreds of letters from those it helped. We are proud of the good work and the charitable donations raised from the news stories Kirsten and the news team did with Zachary.

At the age of three, Zachary got a full-size power wheelchair and was remarkable at operating it. It was a true pleasure for any-one who watched him maneuver the wheelchair through a house, a store, or down the street of our neighborhood. He went shopping, to museums, church, and even raced down the street in his wheelchair. I am sure it was shocking to most to see an eleven-pound kid driving a power wheelchair through a crowd of people. I would walk behind him at a distance and watch the re-action on people's faces. I noticed Zachary would actually respond to different situations with the appropriate manners. If he came upon an elderly person, he would hesitate and/or go around them giving them the right of way they deserved. However, when he came upon others from whom he deserved the right of way, he could part a crowd in a hurry as he forced his way through!

I remember the day he made his debut at church with his new wheelchair. There was a children's Bible class occurring and Zachary could see into the room through the full, window-style wall and doors. Zachary proceeded full speed toward the glass wall, and as I began to worry if he was going to stop, he turned the chair sharply sideways at the last two feet and stopped in-stantly to gaze in at the class of children. All activities in the room stopped to check out Zachary's new ride! When he was sure all had seen he zoomed off as fast as he had approached.

I guess Zachary's life was kind of the same as the way he operated his wheelchair. He came and went very fast but he was in complete control in doing so. Zachary was much more than a son to me. He gave me constant inspi-ration and taught me what life is really for. His inspira-tional abilities increased with each day of his life.

Part II

Zachary's Journal

◆ ◆ ◆

Iknew I must document Zachary's life for two simple reasons: so I could reflect upon them later should Zachary no longer be here on earth, and so I could share this gift with others who would not have the opportunity to meet Zachary. I decided to begin a journal of occurrences, lessons, and the miracles Zachary taught us.

The following is the journal I kept to capture some of these. I am certain in addition to these events I have recorded, there are hundreds of untold stories of Zachary's work. I do know that all of Zachary's work was accomplished through the power of God. At the beginning of this journal of occurrences Zachary is three weeks away from being two years of age.

June 11, 2004

While riding in the car Lindsay, Zachary's 12-year-old sister, tells us that she doesn't think Zachary looks so different or bad like everybody says he does. In her eyes he looks normal, just skinny is all. She doesn't see what the other people who don't know him see. Courtney and Derek, Zachary's brother and sister, did not realize that Zachary looked different until we and others told them. In their eyes he was perfectly normal. Sometime earlier they came home from school and said that kids there had seen him and only a few made fun of him later. I told them to thank the kids that paid him compliments and put the ones in their place that made fun of him. They asked what I meant, and I said to "beat up" on any kid that makes fun of Zachary. No need to tolerate this. I made fun of kids and said things that I shouldn't have when I was very young, and in hindsight it would have been good for someone to put me in my place. Obviously, I do not have much tolerance for those who speak poorly of special needs children. I do not think that special needs children and their families should endure insults if they do not wish to.

We often have strangers approach us at restaurants or stores and say how beautiful Zachary is. He especially gets comments on his blue eyes. I usually say how nice that is and that he likes all compliments. I wish Zachary could tell them himself, but he is so cautious and shy of strangers as a result of during his first year of life all strangers were doctors doing things to him he did not like.

Sometimes we have people approach and ask what is wrong with him medically. That is blunt, but I understand and it is a fair question. Molly did not like it so much, but I told her that people are curious and interested, and that can be a good thing, rather than shying away from kids with medical conditions.

I notice that people stare at him when I take him to the store. I don't mind that, I stare at all babies when I see them. Besides that, Zachary stares at people and gives looks too. On occasion, Molly would tell Zachary in a voice that would be overheard, "Zachary, it isn't nice to stare." Usually the person would get the message and walk away with their head down as if they had been scorned. My approach on the many onlookers and questions we get is that I will give much leeway in these public situations up to the point that I am certain that someone is speaking negatively of Zachary. Fortunately, I have never heard such a word spoken of Zachary. I did decide should that occur it would not be overlooked or tolerated. I would not subject my family or especially Zachary to such behavior.

June 13, 2004

Molly and I took Zachary and the other kids to Kansas City for a weekend trip. Zachary had fun at our friend's house, my company picnic, Great Wolf Lodge, and Cabela's outdoor store. He did not sleep well away from home, though it was a good trip for him. He did well in the van. He liked to look at the taxidermy (ducks) at Cabela's.

In the past few months, Zachary has learned to smile for the camera and enjoys his picture being taken. His eyes are sensitive to light, so he still isn't wild about the flash.

After about eight months of dealing with medical and insurance companies, we were finally able to order Zachary a power mobility chair. The insurance company sure fought us and did not want to pay for it. I really had to be a sore thumb and do some legal research to win the game with them. After spending much time in dispute with the insurance company, they finally approved payment of a portion of the wheelchair. I sold my motorcycle to pay for the remainder. By June 25th he should be wheeling around the neighborhood.

June 14, 2004

Zachary took his first "poopy" on the toilet today. He is tired of wearing diapers. He wants his diapers changed often and when I say often, I mean often. We go through a package of 52 diapers about every 2 days. At $16.00 a package it really adds up. As soon as they are just slightly damp he is ready for a new one. I suspect that his thin, tight skin is sensitive to the moisture and this makes him uncomfortable. We spare no expense to make him comfortable and change his diaper when he asks. I figure with all his challenges we need to do all we can to make him as comfortable as possible.

June 18, 2004

Zachary was up with me this morning at 6:00 A.M. He did not want me to go to work today. He was feeling a little sick. Molly and I were reviewing his medical records and he has not been really sick for about eight months–amazing, considering all he is challenged with. I pray he keeps it up. He spent last night playing with his sister Heidi. She passed him in weight at four months of age. They sure love each other. They are not jealous of each other, only the time Molly and I divide between them.

June 24, 2004

Zachary is the strongest person I know. He is 10½ lbs and he tries with all he has to stand up, scoot across the floor, roll over, plus all the therapy his mom does with him. He is no doubt stronger than me. I weigh 133 lbs., and I bench press 245 lbs. That is not as difficult as what Zachary does everyday. Watching him has motivated me. I lift weights about three times a week. Before Zachary, I would motivate myself to lift that final difficult repetition by thinking about something that would anger me. Now with Zachary in my life, I think of his face and desire to accomplish, and I find the strength for that final repetition. I have also increased the amount of weight I lift, even though I am now 33 years old. I believe positive motivation is true motivation.

Living with Zachary is like having an angel from heaven with me at all times. When he looks at me, I feel as if I am looking straight at God. At 10½ lbs, thin skin, poor muscle and bone structure, he humbles me. I have never had a negative thought of him. I can with complete honesty say that I have NEVER been ashamed of him. I could not be more proud of him. No other has had that impact on me. He makes me want to do the word of God instead of serving myself; he inspires me at all times.

I have noticed a common phrase among families of children with special needs. They often refer to their child as their angel. I just assumed that they were trying to be as affectionate as possible, and angel is a very affectionate word. But now I know that they really mean it when they refer to their child as their Angel from God.

The Truth: I have always felt a special bond with Zachary. In a way, I love him more than the other kids. I struggled with that, since the others are my stepchildren. I now have Heidi, who is not a stepchild; it surprised me that I feel the same for her as I do my stepchildren. Zachary still holds a special place with me that is above Heidi too. At least now I know that it is not because the other kids are mine by marriage that I feel different about them versus Zachary. The other day Courtney, Zach's sister, let it slip that she loves Zachary more than any other family member. Once she realized what she had said, she tried to back up and say that she loved us all the same because she knew that was the right thing to say. What a relief to me to hear that I was not the only one that felt that way about Zachary! I am still on the path to figuring out why Courtney and I have these overpowering feelings of love for Zachary. I think the answer will come later.

Wheelchair: Zachary got his power wheelchair yesterday. He loved it. Then we let him ride around the house in it and we controlled it. Grandma and Grandpa came over to see it. Zachary is very proud of the wheelchair. We all went to the church building and let him drive it in the foyer. He mainly wanted to sit in it and look around at first. Then he let out a rambunctious yell and took off by pushing the joystick. The look on his face was of empowerment. With encouragement from mom and me, he drove it around the church building. That evening he made his tour down our neighborhood street. The entire neighborhood came out to see him and clap for him. He knows how to do the forward and stop. Now we need to teach him to steer and back up. Watching him move down the street 30 yards away from me, under his own power, with kids all around him, in an instant he changed from a baby to one of the kids. Molly said he sure looked different all of a sudden.

July 2, 2004

Zach is starting to get comfortable with his wheelchair. I realize how important it was to get him the wheelchair. It will help him develop mentally, being able to move around efficiently on his own. He knows how to work the wheelchair but he is very hesitant on moving it. He gets really shy on it. Each day I notice improvement with his confidence on being able to move around. He does not have a problem understanding how to move the wheelchair, but he does not want to move and interact on it, because he does not know how to interact. Every day he is better at this. That is progress.

He has spent a lot of time at the doctor's office lately. He went to the orthopedic doctor and got fitted with splints. He hates wearing the splints. It took three people to hold him down for the splints. He now has to wear them several hours each day. The doctor did not think he would ever walk and let us know that he has extremely thin bones. That was tough news because there is not much we can do to fix that. He is scheduled for yearly EKG and heart echo tests in two weeks. Hope all is well with his heart. He has been constipated for four days and a suppository finally fixed that. That is a common problem with him.

Last night, I took Zach to the lake with our Labrador retriever, Rock, to do some hiking. He loves such adventures. He rides in the sling carrier on my chest. He gives Rock orders and hand signals and has fun with that. A deer jumped up about 50 yards away in our side view. Zach caught movement out of the corner of his eye and watched the deer run away. His senses reacted the same as mine, I noticed. He has a keen eye and I pray that we will hunt together someday. We eventually will, no matter what; I am just not sure that the hunting field will be here on earth.

We have already gotten to go fishing together a few times. That was great. Especially the day the family all went crappie fishing in the boat. What a perfect day. Thanks for that one.

July 7, 2004

Today is Zachary's second birthday. Last night I stood over his bed and watched him sleep. I said my prayer over him and then thought about his birthday that would be here in one hour; it was 11:00 P.M. I am not the type of person who gets excited about birthdays. I can practically forget my own. Zachary's birthday is different. To me it is a celebration of beating the odds, defying what the doctors say, and celebrating another year that God has given Zachary to us. I was completely excited about his birthday, and anxiously awaited midnight. I thought to myself, this is how we should feel about Christmas when we celebrate the birth of Jesus Christ. Zachary woke up about 2:00 A.M. for one of his nightly feedings and I was the first to tell him happy birthday, what a great feeling that was. We took Zachary and Heidi out for pizza for his birthday. At dark we took them for a wagon ride around the neighborhood. Saturday is his big birthday party. Molly and I are working hard on getting things ready. I hope Zachary is feeling good for his party. Again, I am so thankful for two years with Zachary. He was given two months to live at one time; I guess that wasn't the Lord's will.

July 12, 2004

We had Zachary's birthday party on Saturday. We had about 40 family and friends attend. Even though Zachary was not feeling too good, he was in top spirits for his party. He truly rose to the occasion. Molly brought the balloons and cake into the house that morning and he was turned "on" for the rest of the day. He had a "Barney"-themed party. He was so proud of his cake and balloons. Zachary really did appreciate each guest that was there, especially the kids. He played with them like he had it all planned out. The big event was when he rode his wheelchair into the room when it was time to open presents. He rode in and started opening presents. The other kids helped him open them up. He talked about each present as he opened them and was so thankful for them. Molly did a great job with the party and food. Everyone had a great time.

I was thankful how everyone cares enough to show up for his event. That really meant a lot to me. I was touched how everyone wanted to spend time with Zachary and I watched as he enjoyed every moment of the party. He was so happy!

I am learning as I watch Zachary that life is not about living to be old, getting married, having children, etc. These are the things that so many of us think are our rights here on earth and the primary reason we are here. Zachary has shown me that we are not here for those things. Instead, we are here to serve God, which includes things like doing God's work, spreading God's word, helping others, and learning what God wants each of us to do. **Zachary may never have the chance to be old in age, but he certainly will be old in God's will.** He has done more of God's will in two years than I have in thirty-three years. We need to realize that not everyone is to get married and have kids, and that is all right as long as we are doing God's will while we are here.

I spent much of my life trying really hard at accomplishing things I thought were important. Now that I am older, I realize those things were not that important, and that I have lost time when I could have been doing God's will. The saddest part is that it was all by my choice. I admire people like Zachary who were chosen to carry such a heavy share of doing God's will. What an honor. But when it comes down to it, all of us have the same choice to either do God's work or not.

July 14, 2004

Some days are tougher than others for me to be away from Zach. Mondays are a struggle for me since I have been with Zach all weekend and I am suddenly without him on Monday at work. While at work, I often think about him and wish I were with him. It is difficult to not know how much time I have with Zach, and I don't like being away from him. That makes it hard for me to focus at work. Luckily I do not have to travel and be away from my family as a requirement for my job. I see Zachary everyday. My motivation for working is knowing I am providing for my family and at the end of the day I get to go home and see them. Knowing Molly is taking care of Zach each day at our home is a great feeling. Nobody takes better care of him than mom. Molly gives me the assurance I need while I am away from home.

Tomorrow Zach has his EKG test and I will be there with him. I hope it does not upset him so much that he gets sick as he often does after medical visits. I wonder sometimes if putting him through all the medical visits is helping or hurting him. I consider just letting him enjoy each day and not medically pursue his problems, unless I am certain of the medical treatment. So much of what he has been through medically has not been worthwhile. And then to top that off I have to spend countless hours of my life fighting the insurance company on paying their share of the invoices. The result of that is spending money, losing time with Zach, and getting a lot of stress added to my life.

Still we attempt to decide which options to pursue medically for Zachary's best interest. It is such a balancing act on determining how aggressive to be or not to be with our son. Everything seems to be an unknown and a simple medical decision by us can have devastating effects on Zachary. These decisions pull at us and we pray for some direction on what are the right things to do for him. Molly has built a medical file for Zachary to record medical visits and tests. We refer to it as we continue to ride what seems like a roller coaster of health issues and concerns. Molly does such a great job in educating herself on the many medical concerns that Zachary deals with. She is Zachary's advocate when he is in the hospital and we are both involved in all aspects of care for him.

July 27, 2004

Zachary and the family did some fishing this past weekend. The weather was unseasonably cool and we took advantage of it. Zach is very sensitive to the sun and heat, so a cloudy and cool weekend was enjoyed. We spent some time with my cousin's family who were visiting from Alaska. All of the kids caught catfish and had a great time. I held Zachary and we walked up and down the bank and watched the other kids fishing. The next morning we went to the ponds by my sister's house and the big bass were really biting. Zachary stayed out there all morning and had a lot of fun. Grandpa and I took turns walking him around the pond. Zachary reeled in a three-pound bass and told him goodbye as I released the fish back into the water.

I spent last night away from Zach when I took my cousin bow-fishing. Zachary called me on the phone and is really missing me. I feel like I have been away from him for a week. It has only been a day and a half. I'm thankful I don't have to travel for my work these days.

Zach's heart tests came back normal. I am thankful for that news. He is so strong.

August 2, 2004

Just thinking this morning about Zachary's reaction every day when I come home from work. I enter the house through the garage entry door and when he hears the door (he always hears the door) he yells out "Dadda!!! " I come into the room and his re-action is not elation but rather urgency. He cannot wait for me to come over and pick him up and give him attention. It is like he has been planning out my arrival all day and the moment is finally here. If he is doing something he literally drops it and moves away to let me know he is ready for me and nothing else will get in the way. What a great feeling it is each day to come home to him and for him to keep up the intensity level each day. All relationships should be that way, but unfortunately that is not the case. There are high percentages of times when we cannot drop things and devote complete attention to our relationships. What we can do is prioritize what we should be devoting our attention to. Are two hours of television more important than our kids and spouse each evening? Decide this in advance and when you can, drop those things that are not important and give complete attention to your relationships. The rewards are great. I cannot wait to get home to Zachary today! When I come through the door this evening I may yell out Zachary!!! . . . and beat him to the yell of Dadda!!!

August 13, 2004

Zachary and Heidi are really becoming buddies. Courtney, Lind-say, and Derek are in Phoenix this week visiting grandpa. Zachary misses them but he is really getting tight with Heidi as she develops.

Zachary did an MRI this week and the hospital messed the test up. We may have to re-do the MRI. It's a lot for him to go through again. Yet another decision for us on whether to do it again or not. We decided to go ahead and reschedule.

Zachary is busy helping me train our dog Rock at the lake. He loves to go and watch Rock run, and he gives him orders.

Some thoughts I have: No person should judge another for placing a sick or disabled child in a home or hospital for care. We can't imagine the task unless we are in it. Some may not have the needed abilities and the best decision may be to allow professionals to provide the primary care. I suggest rather than judge a parent for this, you make an effort to help a parent or child in this situation. That time will not be spent in vain or self-serving. Diseases do not discriminate and can inflict children with parents of varying levels of capabilities. How sad it makes me to see a capable parent who gives up though. How happy it makes me to see a parent who does not give up. Even better is a person who assumes the responsibility of caring for another's sick child. I have seen all these happen.

August 24, 2004

Zachary's MRI showed he has a very small pituitary gland. Other than that it looked good. We have decided to give Zachary human growth hormone to promote his growth. He continues to be so resilient despite all his challenges. His general health is great. He just keeps going and his attitude is better than mine. We just need him to grow. He is getting good at making cookies, mixing things in bowls, drawing, driving his wheelchair, throwing balls, and kicking balls. He has so much potential. It amazes me how much of his potential he has utilized. He is maxed out! I wish I would live up to my potential. I know I am not maxed out like he is.

September 20, 2004

I was thinking about how proud I am of Zachary. We are all proud of our kids, no matter what they act like or look like. It seems they are all superstars in our mind. They are the best on the team, the smartest in the class, etc. Some people look at special needs children and probably think, "How can their parents be happy with such a situation?" The answer is this: *Whenever you put your heart and soul into something, it is easy to be proud of it.* To put that into perspective, that saying holds true with other things besides our children. I see people who are completely proud of their automobile. This may be because they work so hard to get it, or it costs a lot of money, or they work so hard to keep it looking perfect by washing and waxing it. But to someone else the car may seem more like something that several people made a lot of money from selling it to the now-proud owner, everyone from the manufacturer, to the shipper, to the dealer, to the financer. And now the owner is stuck making payments: however he is very proud of that car.

All of us as parents should put our heart and soul into raising our children. When I look at Zachary and my other kids, I see complete beauty and perfection in them. It amazes me that once I had kids, how less important my earthly possessions became to me.

I passed a van on the road this weekend that was headed to the OSU football game. In it was a family that included a young man with Down's syndrome. Just by passing by the van and looking into it I could sense that family was so proud of the young man. One of the ladies had her arm around him and you could tell all was good in their lives. Through this passing glimpse into their van I knew that they had put their hearts and souls into caring for him.

September 20, 2004

I took Zachary and the kids to a gun/hunting/fishing expo in Tulsa this weekend. They had a great time and bought knives and diamond rings, each for a dollar. They were so happy. Zachary had a great time looking around and did not want to leave. He sampled fudge, looked at guns, watched hunting videos, and petted some pointer puppies. It was a busy day and he is becoming more and more like one of the big kids. I know he is really starting to feel like a big kid, I can tell by the way he acts. The only difference is we have to carry him around and feed him bottles of milk.

The other day Molly was brushing Courtney's hair and Zachary watched that and decided he wanted his hair brushed to. He scooted right over and backed up to Molly for his turn. Molly brushed his hair and told him how good it looked and he really enjoyed the treatment. The funny thing is that you can count his hairs he has so few. He doesn't really realize that though. He thinks he has a full head of hair. In fact, he doesn't think there is anything wrong with him. What a great attitude. He sure does love his mom.

September 21, 2004

Zachary really tries hard to imitate me. Last night I was working on his wheelchair and he wanted to use the screwdriver so he could also work on something. He found a screw on one of his cars and went to work. He then attempted to fix his Barney and Baby Bop dolls. I guess something needed to be fixed with them. He wants to do everything like me. I better set a good example for him.

October 7, 2004

Last night from out of nowhere Zachary's brother, Derek, asked when we check to see if our home smoke detectors work. I told him we should do it monthly but it had been a while so we need to do it and thanked him for reminding me. He went on to ask if every room had a detector. I told him all the bedrooms and kitchen did. He said that if for some reason that the rest of the family escaped outside during a fire and he was left in his room that he would check and see if Zachary was in his room and if so he would save him. I told him that was the right thing to do and that he needed to look out for his brother. He added that if Zachary were on fire, he would jump on him and roll on him to put it out. Derek's statements amazed me. Without being encouraged, he had offered to save Zachary and even suffer personal harm or give up his life in doing so. I immediately hugged him and told him how proud I was of him. I am sure that when I was age seven, I was more worried about what possessions I would try to save in the event of a fire. Do I grab my toys, my money bank, my photographs, etc? It seems Derek is further along than I was at that age. Zachary has had an impact on Derek, and made

Derek appreciate how precious life and what we do with our lives is. Derek's conversation with me was evidence of a seven-year-old's sincere love for his brother.

October 11, 2004

Courtney and Derek were doing push-ups in the living room for exercise. Zachary and I were watching them. Zachary decided he also needed to try some push-ups. He rolled onto his stomach and with my help he tried his hardest to do them. He made me count like I had counted for Courtney and Derek. He got tired at about twenty and quit. After about a thirty-second pause he was ready to go again. He laughed with each repetition. Then when finished he insisted that I do some pushups. He watched with approval and then wanted help doing another set.

I watched him on the floor last night playing on a blanket. He was not wearing clothes in preparation for his pajamas. I looked at him and thought about what a miracle it was that in spite of his failure to grow physically, he continues to develop in his physical and mental skills. Even though his muscles and bones have not advanced in development, even though he has not gained a single pound in the past year, Zachary continues to grow in his abilities. How does he do it? I watch him every day overcome challenges and push his limits. His encouragement comes from within. He strives to satisfy, impress, and make me happy with his every action. All of this even though he has not been given the body that many of us take for granted. Zachary does not come up with excuses; instead, he produces results.

I think of how many times I have let excuses get in the way of the things I should be doing. Things like: if I had more time, if I had more money, if I was a better speaker, if I was a smarter, if I was stronger . . .

All of us can come up with personal limitations, some more severe than others. We need to not focus on our limitations and how they are keeping us from accomplishing God's work. Instead, we should be producing good deeds through God's will by:

- making an attempt;
- doing the hard work;
- prioritizing our work;
- overcoming challenges;
- believing.

Remember that there is always ability for growth and spiritual advancement in our lives, no matter what the circumstances. Sometimes the worst situations present the best opportunities for growth.

October 21, 2004

I took all the kids out to the lake for the evening. Zachary was in charge of the dog and he insisted on opening the kennel and telling him when to get out of the truck. We trained Rock and Zachary directed him into a covey of quail. Zach was really pleased when the covey of quail exploded into the treetops and across a field. I looked at his face and he was smiling as the birds buzzed away. We hiked across fields and woods and saw deer and followed the trails. Zachary kept an eye on everyone to make sure we stayed together. Zachary watched a flock of geese fly the lake's edge and alerted me to their presence. Nothing passes without Zachary noticing. He now knows me so well he is able to bring things to my attention that he knows are of my interest. It was a nice evening.

November 1, 2004

What do we want for our kids? To be the best on the team, grow up and be happily married to someone wealthy, get a college education, stay close to home, etc.? What we really should want and be striving towards for them is the same thing God wants for them, to get to heaven. Are we focusing our child-raising efforts on that or something else? If Zachary dies young he will go to heaven. The Bible tells me so. There is peace in knowing that for me. If our kids make it to an age where they become keepers of their salvation, will we have done our part as parents to prepare them?

Additionally, I believe that many of the parenting challenges and/or hardships that are encountered can be endured, resolved, or avoided altogether if you raise your children with these things in mind.

November 16, 2004

Molly is working hard to get Zachary a service dog to help him with tasks and mobility. Most service dog organizations will not place dogs with individuals younger than five years of age. Southwest Service Dogs of Clarksville, Arkansas made an exception for Zachary. Molly's persistence and Zachary's persuading smile could not be refused. Zachary has had two visits from the potential service dogs now. He really likes the dogs. He sometimes points out the window into the backyard and says that he saw Lamy or Hobbs out there. That is wishful or hopeful thinking, I guess. He tries to convince us and then smiles to let us know he was teasing. This is his way of telling us what he wants by making it a game or perhaps a scheme. He knows how to get what he wants.

Zachary has now been in the *Stillwater News Press* and *Daily Oklahoman,* and has appeared on News 9 television to promote awareness for Southwest Service Dogs and The Progeria Research Foundation. He was recognized by a lady while shopping at the store last night. She said she saw his picture in the Sunday paper. She reached out and touched his head affectionately. She seemed happy to meet him and Molly.

December 13, 2004

The family went to the Shriners' Christmas party in Tulsa yesterday. Zachary sure had fun, although he was not too sure about those clowns. He watched them but did not want them to talk to him. He did enjoy all the gifts and the other kids there. He was quite popular since everyone had seen him on television or in the newspaper. Lots of people wanted to meet him. Molly and I were proud of him and also proud of the way our other kids treated the other "patient children" at the party. The Shriners put on a great event that really meant a lot to the families there. Zachary was so tired after the party but still wanted to go visit grandma and papa Moore. That night he slept all the way home.

Zachary has so many friends that care about him. Knowing this makes me so proud of him and also proud of my fellow man for being so caring and giving. People in all sorts of situations have responded to Zachary and sent money to Southwest Service Dogs or The Progeria Research Foundation. Zachary receives letters every day, from all over the country, and from all ages. He receives letters from kids in foster homes who write about how they wish their former parents had loved them the way Zachary's parents love him for what he is. He receives letters and cards from entire cellblocks of the penitentiary at Leavenworth, Kansas. These are from convicted felons who write that they are brought to tears at the strength Zachary has shown. He has money sent for the service dog by kids who break open their piggy banks and send all they have. We try to do special responses for kids that do that type of thing. Zachary gets biblical scriptures sent to him. He has Oklahoma State University students doing fundraisers on his behalf to help fund Southwest Service Dogs and The Progeria Research Foundation.

December 21, 2004

On Friday, Hobbs the service dog arrived at our house for a visit. One could not script a more affectionate moment. Zachary looked up and saw Hobbs and began to yell for him with elation. He put his arms up for a hug and began to frantically scoot over to him at full speed. He gave Hobbs a hug and turned and exclaimed to us all "Hobbs was his puppy"! Zachary was excited, full of love, and proud all at the same time. I could not keep the tears back. It was more than I could handle to see him so happy. I thought to myself, all the work and money Zachary's friends have donated for Hobbs was absolutely worthwhile. I wish every one of them could have seen this moment. I want all to know it could not have been more special for us and exceeded all my expectations. Hobbs means so much to Zachary and in the four days Hobbs has been with him for a visit, Zach is happier, more confident, and most importantly he is blessed to have a dog dedicated to him who he loves so much. I am grateful for all the friends that care so much about Zachary and have helped him and Southwest Service Dogs. Hobbs goes back tomorrow for more training and we hope he will complete training in early spring. Zachary will get to visit Hobbs during this training time.

On Sunday, Zachary had the Oklahoma County Sheriff's Department come and deputize him, his brother, sisters, and Hobbs. The kids had so much fun. He particularly liked the uniform they made for him. He did not want to take it off, not even for bed that night. They also modified his wheelchair with sirens and lights. When Zachary was presented the honorary deputy certificate, Hobbs was by this side. The crowd cheered when Hobbs used his paw to shake the hand of the Sheriff when the award was presented. He ended the ceremony with a ride in the sheriff's car with the sirens on. He was so proud of being recognized by them. Everyone at the ceremony made the news and it was a great story. It was great to know that Zach has so many friends who care about him. It was obvious the Oklahoma County Sheriff's office is a true friend to Zachary. I could tell they all cared so much for Zachary and it meant so much to me. We plan to visit them soon.

January 1, 2005

The *Daily Oklahoman* front page listed the biggest stories/quotes for 2004 in Oklahoma. Amongst all the negative or shocking stories was a photo of Zachary and a quote from me "I feel as if I am looking directly into the eyes of God when I look at Zachary." It was nice to know Zachary provided a positive story of inspiration amongst all the negative headlines.

About my quote: Zachary has overcome so much and is so strong that I do feel like I cannot and should not do wrong in his presence. He truly is a gift and a miracle from God, and I somehow feel such a strong spiritual presence through him. At such a young age and by such simple means, Zachary is doing so much of God's work that I am humbled by him. It definitely pushes me to do more of God's work by my own actions. We can all be inspired by others who are doing God's work.

January 11, 2005

Zach is very interested in guns and archery and tries to draw the older kids' bow back. I need to rig some special gear and get some good weather so I can get him started. I let him fire off the BB gun in the backyard for now. I also take him hiking, and he watches for deer and quail. He started fishing last year. Zach is only ten pounds and Molly understands but thinks I am crazy, but I am not going to later regret things I did not get to do with him. We have fun every day, no matter what! He drives my truck around the neighborhood, cooks on the charcoal grill, flips pancakes, makes cookies, and helps me make lattés in the morning.

I hope that I will never forget what his laughs sound like, or more importantly, how they make me feel. He laughs so often, it makes me confident that he is happy and that Molly and I are doing a great job in raising him. I know he is in pain and discomfort, but he continues to be happy. He is so strong and has so much desire to be happy.

January 20, 2005

Zachary has grown 1½ inches in 2½ months. That is an accomplishment for him. We are so excited and pray he will keep growing. These days I spend as much time as I can trying to help Zachary interact with his brothers and sisters and play. He is very limited in his mobility but has such a huge desire to interact. I spend most every moment of my evening holding him in the palm of my hand so that his feet touch the floor and he feels like he is walking around on his own. He wants to get into things, open/close doors, play with his brother and sisters, move from room to room, climb onto furniture, and look out the windows. All these things are so important in the mental development of a child. It is a fine line I walk on helping him. Should I continually help him to do these things or should I push him to do more things on his own? There are so many things he can't do on his own it is tough for me to not help him. For instance, while he can scoot from room to room, it takes him so long that when he finally gets there the reason he went there has already moved on or the moment is over. He struggles to keep up with siblings as they play throughout the house. Even Heidi crawls too fast for him. His electric wheelchair is great but is too big to maneuver everywhere and once he gets somewhere he can't grab what he wants because the base of the chair won't let him get close. Besides that, it is not practical for him to remain in the chair for long periods of time and he can't get in and out of it himself. So for now I will hold him in the palm of my hand out in front of me so that he doesn't even notice I'm there and let him play throughout the house and do things "on his own" with a little help from dad. In return, I get to watch him be "the Boss" and I get a great bicep workout. I don't mind a bit spending my non-work time helping and playing with Zachary. I know I will never regret a single moment spent with him. And there certainly is nothing on television better or any other activity as fun as my Zachary time.

January 24, 2005

It was a busy weekend with Zachary. Friday evening was especially warm so I spent it with Zachary and the other kids outside. We went on a walk and then went back inside for diaper changes. Zach looked out the back window and insisted that he go out there and play on the swing. So he and Heidi stayed busy on the swing until dark. The next day it was watching Derek's basketball game. Zach watches and wants to run out on the court and play so bad. He can't hardly stand to just watch, he wants to play. We went to church on Sunday. He knows to insist on going to the children's nursery so he can play. Of course I have to stay with him. He has so much fun attending church. Sunday evening we have the neighbors over for dinner. He plays hard wanting to move from room to room and checking on everybody there.

Rock (our dog) is sick and we are letting him sleep inside. It makes me laugh to hear Zachary call him. He says his name and then makes a kissing sound over and over.

January 26, 2005

I came home from work yesterday and Zachary let out his usual yell of "Daddy!" when he heard the door open! What a great feeling! I came in and said hello to all the kids. I went to the other room to change clothes, and I could hear Zachary scooting his way across two rooms and into my bedroom. He was smiling big when I made eye contact with him. He immediately turned and picked up the pace and then started laughing to let me know I was supposed to chase him. I obliged him and caught up with him on my hands and knees. I tapped him on the back and he squealed with laughter. This is a normal routine for him and I love it. I picked him up and he laid his head on me to show his love while I toured him around the house. We picked up Heidi along the way and then at Zach's request proceeded from room to room to find Courtney, Derek, and Momma. It sure feels good to have kids that get that excited when you get home every day. Any plans I had on accomplishing tasks that are non-kid related suddenly get put on the back burner. But that's all right and I proved that to myself today. I looked at a picture of Zachary taken when he was seven months old. I thought to myself about that time in his life; it wasn't that long ago, only two years, but he sure has changed. I would give a great deal to be able to be in that moment again with him and just hold him at that age. Then I think how I will feel once the kids are completely grown. I compare all these feelings with how I feel about those non-kid tasks that I have accomplished in the past. There are few of those tasks that I long to re-live the way I do for those moments with my kids. That is how I know my priorities are in line.

That brings us to the balance of providing *for* your kids and providing love to your kids. It is a difficult balance for us all. How many hours a day should I work, how much time should I spend working on the lawn, how much time should I spend doing my hobbies that keep me sane, and how much time should I spend alone with my wife. These are all daily decisions for many of us. Certainly all or most of these things require a certain amount of our time so we can truly provide for our family. I don't think there is any exact formula that will calculate the balance for us. Instead, I suggest that we look at indicators. For example:

- Am I able to provide my family with the objects and environment they need and the opportunities they deserve?
- Do I have a happy relationship with my kids and wife?
- Are my kids excited to see me when I get home?
- Do my kids want to do activities with me?

Everyone should come up with their own indicators that are pertinent to them.

February 4, 2005

Molly is in Dallas on a business trip and Grandma and Grandpa Moore are taking care of the kids. Zachary and the kids really enjoy the attention. After they spent a couple of days with Zachary, I asked them if they felt he acted like a normal kid. They agreed with me that he did not act normal. When you spend time with Zachary, you get a sense that he is living on an accelerated schedule and that he knows it. He tries to do as much as possible in a day and is always "on." It seems there is no "downtime."

Even throughout the night he wakes up and wants attention from us. I can wake up with him, and he will never even open his eyes; he just gets a new diaper and some bottle, and then he wants me to walk him around the house. He will be practically asleep while I am walking him, and I can squeeze him with a hug and he will let out a laugh. Such happy behavior in the middle of the night seems uncommon to me, but it is normal for him. He utilizes every possible moment in a positive way. As for me, I am working harder to spend all my moments in a positive way.

February 7, 2005

Zach was sick over the weekend. He started coughing on Friday and just wanted to lie around. Every time this happens the thoughts enter my mind that maybe this is the illness that will do him in. His health is so fragile that I can't help but think of this possibility. I get stressed out thinking that I had better drop what I am doing and pour all my attention to him. Then I reflect and think about the day before and how I might have to live with the memories of that day spent with Zachary as the last one he had healthy for the rest of my life. Thank God again, that by Sunday he was feeling better. His cough had mostly ended, and he seemed energized once again. God has given him remarkable resilience. I have been through this scenario more times than I can remember with Zach. Each time I give God all the glory for Zach's health. I pray daily for Zach's continued health, and I ask God to show me His will for the way I spend my time with Zach. Then it is up to me to do God's will.

Today he prepares for the arrival of Hobbs, his service dog. Hobbs will visit for one week and then return for one month of final training. Zach is so excited. He has called me on the phone to let me know Hobbs is on the way and that when I get home from work he will show me!

February 21, 2005

I took Zach and Heidi to Boomer Lake to walk the trail today. They had great fun in the stroller. We let Rock practice his retrieves for a while, and they both clapped for him. Zach was so excited to go over the wooden bridge and see the ducks. He waved and said bye to the ducks as we strolled away.

It is so hard for me to put him down to sleep each night. Every time I do, the thought crosses my mind that this may be the last time

I see him alive. I constantly wake up at night to check on him. I always want to make sure that I take a good look at him since it seems so possible it may be the last. After 2 1/2 years, I still have not gotten used to this routine. Through my faith I have complete happiness in our situation though. I know that I would not do anything different. I constantly analyze our actions to ensure I maintain a course that I won't later regret. I always come back to the core elements of why we are all here. I remember what those are and realize that is exactly what Zachary is doing. I cannot say that for myself, certainly not all the time. So with that in mind, I know Zachary is doing what God wants him to be doing. That is what matters. These days the only sadness I get about our situation with Zach is the fact that if he leaves us soon, I will not have my "in the flesh" spiritual guide. And that is a selfish thought, so I do not let that keep me sad, but instead I rejoice in whatever time I have with Zachary.

March 1, 2005

Last night I called him Mr. Moore. It seems appropriate; I have so much respect for him. Zach looks back at me like it was fine with him, too. He prefers "Boss," though.

It is very important to me Zachary spend as much time as possible with his grandparents. I hope so much they will have a relationship with Zach close enough that they know how wonderful he really is. This is only gained if you spend a lot of time with him. Only then can you truly appreciate his abilities and desire. Lately my parents have said things to me to make me think they finally understand those things with Zachary. I find much happiness in their knowing how great Zachary truly is.

Molly's dad, who only sees Zachary about once a year, seemed very impressed this weekend when Zachary made him a cappuccino with fresh-ground coffee beans. Zachary knows every step of the process and is so proud when the drink is prepared.

On February 25th Hobbs came to stay with Zachary, thanks to the continual good work of Kate Morgan at Southwest Service Dogs and the generosity of Zachary's many friends. He is so happy with him. Southwest Service Dogs received donations from many of our family and friends—some in Oklahoma, some in other states, some strangers, some motivated organizations and businesses, and my employer. The list is impressive, and I am proud of my fellow man.

Zachary and Hobbs' story made the television news and the front page of the Daily Oklahoman newspaper. Molly even bought a cake with a picture of Zachary and Hobbs on it and it said "Zachary and Hobbs, Together Forever". His celebrity status continues.

March 9, 2005

Zachary was honored with a party at Oklahoma State University. There was a big turnout, and the girls who organized the party, Amber and Kate, did a great job. They had cake, food, drinks, a bubble machine, a Barney costume, and dozens of cards that were made for Zachary. He played with the bubble machine but did not like the Barney costume. He was a bit scared of it and told me it was not really Barney. Can't fool him, I guess.

I was amazed at how many people made their way up to Zachary and me to tell us how much they admired Zachary or how he inspired them. Many of them wanted to interact with him to see what he was like. Zach did great mingling with everyone. He made lots of new friends that night. Zachary truly is the "big man on campus" in spite of his small physical size. It seems everyone knows who he is, and his party most certainly was the "place to be" that night.

I watched people at the party keep an eye on Zachary and wait for their opportunity to approach him to say hello. Some of the shy people in attendance noticeably wanted to meet him. I tried to make sure they all had a chance to talk with Zachary. Some who had prepared cards wanted to have the card read by Zachary, Molly, and me, so they could see our reaction. That meant a lot to me. I really felt all in attendance truly loved Zachary.

I was asked to speak at the party. I informed the group about Zachary, progeria, The Progeria Research Foundation, and Southwest Service Dogs. I then told a story about Zachary and related it to how great an event and fundraising effort the people there had done.

I am so proud of the Oklahoma State University students and how they genuinely care for Zachary.

March 30, 2005

Though she is perfectly healthy, Heidi has it tougher than Zach. He has already been given the gift of salvation. When I look at Heidi, I see a normal child. She will likely go through the struggles I'm going through to find salvation. Zach is more like an angel in our presence. When I look at Zach, I don't see a struggling 10-pound, 2½-year-old boy. I see a person who is complete in God's will. Zachary is not working for himself and his own salvation; he is working for others.

March 31, 2005

The Oklahoma County Sheriff's department called today. They are doing Zachary a big favor and we were coordinating it. I thanked them and he said they were glad to help and that "he is our boy". That really impacted me to think they care so much for Zachary to call him their own. It was a great thing to say, and I know they mean it based on their actions. They have his photographs framed on their office walls at the Sheriff's Department. They call for updates on him all the time. They want to see him as often as possible. They really care about him and continue to do so.

Zachary made a visit to the jail, and he was able to do one of his favorite things. That is to open and close doors. He had the ultimate control this day, because he was able to open and close the jail door while the prisoners came and went. When the prisoners looked over and saw Zachary sitting on the counter and pushing the door's button, they seemed very surprised. Some smiled and some just seemed confused when they saw him. I was amused, because Zachary just thought he was helping everyone out by doing this task.

April 4, 2005

Zachary was the Grand Marshal at the Shriners' Circus in Oklahoma City this past weekend. It was an amazing experience. The Shriners really made it special for Zachary. What a wonderful organization. We met so many Shriners who told us how much they loved us and would do anything for us. I was amazed at how many people wanted to meet Zachary—everybody from the head of the Shriners to the guy selling cotton candy in the stands. During intermission there was a group of people ten deep waiting to meet Zachary: moms who wanted their kids to meet Zach, business leaders who wanted to offer help with Zachary's fundraising for PRF and Southwest Service Dogs, Shriners who knew Zach and wanted to say hello, and other Shriners who had heard and read about him and wanted to meet him. People were so pleased when I told them to shake his hand. Other people would sneak a touch of his arm or head, and you could see they were so pleased to do so. We had people tell us they had all his newspaper articles cut out and photos on their office wall for inspiration. Comments were made like "now I can tell everyone I met Zachary in person." I knew how many people responded to the story at the time it ran, but I had no idea how many people were still following Zachary's story and remained interested in him. It makes me so incredibly happy to know Zachary is doing such good work. This was another experience that answers the question of why God would allow such an illness to occur in a child. It's no mystery to me; Zachary is one of God's soldiers here on earth. I am so pleased to be able to witness such good work.

Zachary really enjoyed the elephants, dogs, and horses at the circus. He clapped and laughed through the entire performance. He really liked being able to get within a few feet of the elephant and look into its eye. He also liked all the attention he was given. The Shriner clowns were practically fighting over who got to entertain him. He was assigned his own personal clown for the circus. During the circus the clowns used his name in their performance. Zachary thought that was funny.

April 5, 2005

Zachary is really into walking these days. Heidi started walking, and he wants to do the same. He walks by me holding him by the bottom or under his arms and supporting most of his weight. He can support his own weight for about ten seconds. His contractures make it impossible for him to walk on his own. He sure won't be told that though. He demands I help him walk all around the house, garage, and yard. He wants to walk on the kitchen countertops, furniture, windowsills, etc. He does this for hours or until my knees and arms give out. He wears me out doing this, but how can I say no when he pleads with me to help him walk as he sees Heidi take off across the floor. It does not seem fair to say no, and it makes him so happy. When I grab him and he starts walking, he will let out a scream of amusement. These times really make me wish he could walk on his own. However, I don't think negatively for this. Instead I am thankful his mind and body are telling him to want and to try to walk. This desire is what keeps him so healthy. Even though he can't accomplish everything, he clearly wants to. He is so fortunate to have the capability to try and the potential to one day walk. I believe one day he will be able to walk on his own. If not, that is all right too; the desire he has to do so will serve him in so many other ways.

April 18, 2005

This was a big weekend for Zachary. We attended a wedding, and at the reception they had a western theme party. Zachary danced to every song. You couldn't get him off the dance floor. The look on his face was memorable, to say the least. I watched him dancing in Molly's arms. He clapped his hands and smiled at me. As he danced next to and with the other kids, I knew he felt so equal. He wanted to have fun just like them, and he sure did. I will never forget him dancing in Molly's arms to a song and smiling at me. I helped him walk out there to do a "line dance." He did great and was able to follow along with the others. It really surprised me how well he did.

The next day we went fishing at the lake. Zachary drove the boat and managed the fish in the boat's fish livewell. We caught several crappie, and he had to be involved in everything that happened. He loves to drive the boat and look around at the wildlife. I was surprised at how much confidence he has gained since last year. He will touch the fish now and doesn't mind if the water splashes him. Zachary has his own tackle box filled with lures of many brilliant colors. The more colorful the lure the better he likes them. I let him choose which color of lure he fishes with. He is so pleased when his selection of lure produces a fish. After a period of catching fish, he was content to scooting around the deck of the boat and organizing his tackle box over and over again. Each lure must be in its proper spot in the tackle box. I laughed when I turned around to see him sitting next to his tackle box and picking lures out one by one and quickly throwing them overboard into the water! Apparently he decided it was fun to do this mischievous act, or perhaps he decided he did not like a particular color lure anymore and desired to get rid of it, or maybe he just thought the fish were hungry! I don't know for sure what he was thinking but he sure was having fun. When I hollered his name and asked what he was doing he let out a laugh and began to throw the lures into the water faster than ever! A gentle wrestling match broke out as I grabbed him and tried to persuade him to not throw all our lures into the water unless they were tied onto our fishing line. It was all part of the fun we have when we fish together. Truth be told, I would let him throw everything we own into the lake if it made him happy. He had a great evening at the lake and did not want to go home.

April 22, 2005

Zachary is having a big week at the lake camping. He loves to be out in the boat and playing in the camper trailer. He watches the birds and waves at them. He and Heidi both went out in the boat yesterday. Molly and I had our hands full taking care of them while they were in the boat. They sure had fun, though. Zachary stayed at camp until 11:00 P.M., and then he was ready for his own bed.

I can't help but feel a constant sense of urgency for making Zachary happy. I feel guilty if I am not with him. It is hard to enjoy the other things in life that I do without him. I have made a real effort to center all of my life on him. It is a balancing act trying to do things with his brother and sisters. Molly and I often sacrifice any plans we would have together in an effort to fit in more time with Zachary. The good thing is, it is so rewarding doing things with him. He gives us so much in return that we never regret anything that we did not do as a result of being with him. I know we will feel the same later when we look back. That is what keeps us both going each day and each night.

May 2, 2005

People seem to be drawn to Zachary. Many want to meet him and truly care for him. When I think about Zach's situation and try to assess how bad it is or isn't, I compare it to other situations. Such as children killed in car wrecks or other sudden accidents, sons and daughters who are killed in combat, and many other things that are the headlines of our current news. People care about those individuals too, but I guess the difference is those situations come and go somewhat quickly. These tragic occurrences are sudden and unforeseen. Is Zachary's situation more tragic? I don't think so. Zachary's condition is more like one of those accidents in slow motion that can be witnessed by all those who see him. Further, people have the ability to tell him they love him while he is still with us, and they do all the time. Everywhere we go some person comes up and tells Zach they love him. Sometimes they tell him with those exact words and sometimes with their actions. It is a wonderful thing for Zachary and that person. Wouldn't it be great if everybody treated children or even adults with that attitude? The attitude that they deeply care about this person and want to tell them or show them they love them because they may not get another chance. Do you treat your children this way? How about the rest of your family, friends, or even people you meet? It is a wonderful thing to see and be with Zachary and witness this everyday.

May 9, 2005

Zachary's big vacation to Branson, Missouri was so much fun. Molly planned out lots of fun stuff for us to do. We watched the Dixie Stampede show, and Zachary loved the animals. He sat up tall and clapped and waved. He really enjoyed the food and the excitement.

We also went to Silver Dollar City and Zachary was on the go all day. He wanted to do everything. To my surprise, he did not say "no" to any ride at the theme park. He has no fear of heights. I took him up on the Tom Sawyer jungle gym ride, and he waved back down to everyone. He also rode the carousel and watched several shows.

We fed trout at the fish hatchery, looked at the butterfly exhibit (a little bit hot/humid), and he really enjoyed the Bass Pro Wildlife Museum. He was excited to see ducks, fish, otters, and bobcats. He understands which animals are predators, and he does not want to get close to those. Things like a very large catfish, alligators, and sharks. He only wants to see those at a distance.

He was able to keep up for three full days. Heidi was not so lucky. She was really run down at the end of each day. But she woke up in the morning ready to go again. The big kids loved the cabin we stayed in. They had their own rooms and thought it was great.

Molly and I had fun watching Zachary. He was so appreciative and enjoyed every minute of the vacation like it was the best ever. He gets so much enjoyment out of life. He is excited and enthused about everything. I like nothing better than watching him have fun. This was surely the most memorable trip for us all.

May 11, 2005

As I watch Zachary these days, it is apparent he wants so much to be like others and do the things others do. He has such a strong desire to do the things his brother and sisters are doing, things like walking, dancing, playing on the backyard swing, going on amusement park rides, and riding a bicycle. I try to remember that desire when I am around other disabled people, and I use this knowledge to guide my actions. I do things like:

- talking about things they are able to do or relate to;
- complimenting them on their capabilities rather than talk about their constraints;
- not asking them about their disabilities, but instead asking them about their abilities;
- treating them as equals;
- not telling them I feel sorry for them, or even worse, that I am sad for them;
- offering to help them as if you were helping anyone else, the way I would help a person with their hands full of packages trying to open a door;
- remembering that a person with a life-long disability is not likely experiencing the same feelings as someone who was just recently diagnosed with an illness or disability. They likely are quite bored with discussing the problem with every person they meet.

May 16, 2005

Lately when I think about Zachary and ask why he is the way he is and analyze how he is able to deal with it, I come up with this: On one hand he is like an angel sent from heaven to do God's work. But then when I analyze the situation and compare with others, I realize all of us could be the same as he is.

We all deal with tragedy, hardship, pain, suffering, and eventually death. Zach's life is not different than ours. He may have more pain than the average person. He may die sooner than the average person. The key word is *average*. That does not mean he will have the most painful and shortest life. There are no "guaranteed rates" in these areas of life. There are no guidelines on what is fair in life. We all are going to experience these things. We all experience life and death. The only thing we can control is what we do with the situations we are faced with. The length of our lives is a certain unknown. That is why it is so important to do God's work now! If Zachary and others like him are doing God's work so diligently so can all of us. God wants us all to do His work. God wants us to be successful. It does not matter what your current status in life is, whether you are suffering from illness, busy with your career, fighting in a war, living in a war-stricken town, or serving time in prison. The list goes on and on, and you need to ask yourself what is your status? Is it so busy that you do not have time for God? I struggle with this every day and with my every action, especially when I consider how easy a life I currently have.

June 10, 2005

Zachary spent twelve days in the hospital and got out June 3rd. He likely had a virus that became pneumonia. His lung capacity was poor, and it was a struggle for him to breathe. He did not have much energy at all for the first eight days. The doctors warned us he might not make it through this illness, and by looking at him I certainly believed them. They flew him by emergency helicopter from Stillwater to Tulsa when he became sick.

Molly and I stayed with him the entire time at the hospital. That was all he asked for while he was there. Zachary had lots of visitors, and we all prayed for him. We did not sleep the first five days we were at the hospital. The nights were long, and it appeared Zach would not make it through each of those first five nights in the hospital. We tried to take turns watching over him, but I would just lay there listening to him struggle to breathe while I was supposed to be sleeping.

On about the ninth day, Zach started to show improvement. Prayers were being answered. Zach tried so hard each minute he was in the hospital. Even at times when he was very weak, I could play with him and make him smile and laugh. His attitude never diminished. He was a much better patient than I would have been. He obviously was using God given strength to maintain each breath and an inspiring attitude. He was mentally doing better than I was at the hospital, almost as if he was trying to pull

Molly and I through this experience. Molly and I both fed off his positive attitude. Molly had only four hours total sleep in six days at the hospital. She amazed me, and I have no doubt her dedication kept Zachary going. This was just another peak to her three years of care she has given to Zachary.

I certainly had an outpouring of emotions during his illness. I was just as emotional with joy when he got to go home. I watched Zachary ride his power wheelchair down the hall, into the elevator, and out the hospital doors. He leaped with exhilaration when he saw our truck pulling up to get him. I will never forget how it felt to take Zachary home that day. But even in this moment of triumph I worried about when we would be entering the hospital doors again.

Since Zachary has been home, we have not wasted time enjoying him. We picked right back up with as many of our activities as his health would allow. He is still not back 100% but his desire has always been at 100%.

The thing I was the saddest about losing if Zachary did not make it was his ability to do God's work by impacting other people in his desire to be good despite his physical limitations. I have cherished that as I watched him continue this since he has gotten better. Some of these moments include:

- watching all the patients and families stand in the halls of the children's hospital and cheer as he rode his power wheelchair around the hospital after being near the point of death days earlier.
- watching as child patients and nurses at the hospital kissed him goodbye and told him they loved him so much.
- holding him as he met and shook hands with Kyle Maynard. Kyle happened to be in Stillwater for induction into the Wrestling Hall of Fame for his courageous actions in the sport of wrestling. Kyle was born with no limbs and has managed to succeed in sports. More importantly Kyle has been able to spread a message of inspiration to thousands of people. He is a hero to our

family, and it was an honor to meet him and his dad. Zachary and Kyle were instant friends and Zach used both hands to shake Kyle's limb. I was so proud to be there to see that moment, and I will never forget it. This meeting happened on Zach's first day home from the hospital.

- seeing him interact with people he met at the mall and restaurant one evening. Some of the people would walk up and ask if he was Zachary Moore. They were so pleased to meet him.
- watching him meet all the workers at the G&H Duck Decoy facility during our visit there.
- reading the many "get well" cards he received.

June 16, 2005

When I consider the three years of Zachary's life and try to sum up the experience, it amazes me. While there have been some tough times for Zachary, all I can think about is all the fun we've had and, more importantly, all the good work he has accomplished. I think about all the laughter we shared, places he has been, friends he has made, and people he has inspired. He even managed to do these things during hospital stays. His attitude has never faltered.

While we do strive for better health for him, we love the person he is. Our experience with Zachary has left me with no complaints. Zachary is happy, and so is his family. He has inspired me to accept life's tragedies or hardships; it is merely part of living. Everybody will experience these things, and it will not be our choice to do so. It is our choice, however, how we manage our life when and after these things occur. The decisions to our choices are simple. It is the actions of these decisions that often come difficult to us. Zachary is living proof that if you follow God's way, you will be rewarded with happiness, for Zachary is always happy.

June 22, 2005

One of my biggest fears the first year of Zachary's life was that other people would not know how wonderful a child he is. I witnessed this every day, and I was afraid that others, due to his appearance or diagnosis, would not be able to see this wonderful child for what he really is. Now he is almost three years old and has hundreds of friends who deeply care about him and truly love and admire him.

It started with his grandparents and other family, and then spread to neighbors, and now to a diversity of people. It is very satisfying to me knowing so many other people are able to see what I see in him and what God has given him.

Molly and I do not question why this has happened to Zachary or us. We don't hold God responsible for inflicting Zachary with tragedy or have any anger about his illness. The moment Molly went into labor eight weeks early, I prayed God would help us through and give us a child to love.

When Zach was born and in intensive care for five weeks, we prayed for strength for Zachary, us as his parents, and the nurses and doctors caring for him. When we later realized he might have long-term problems and a life-threatening condition, we prayed for more strength and let God know how thankful we were for Zachary, no matter what his physical condition and life span.

All of these prayers have been answered. Molly and I understand God has blessed us with all our children. We don't pray that Zachary will be miraculously cured by God. Instead we pray for the strength and knowledge it takes for us to care for him and for the strength and knowledge and motivation of scientists, doctors, and others who are developing treatments and cures for his condition. We pray and let God know how thankful we are for another day, another moment with Zachary and our other children.

We believe God has answered our prayers when another parent of a child with progeria, Dr. Leslie Gordon, began The Progeria Research Foundation, when a research scientist retains motivation to spend day after day performing research to find a cure, when people make sacrifices to give help in funding these works, when people show kindness and love to Zach making him spiritually healthy. Prayers are being answered!

July 18, 2005

Zach's third birthday party was a success. We had over one hundred guests at his birthday party. Rather than Zachary getting too many gifts, we asked that donations be made to The Progeria Research Foundation. We raised $2,400 for The Progeria Research Foundation.

Zach had fun with everyone there. Before the party started he rode in the News 9 helicopter. The sun and heat did not stop him from getting in the helicopter and going on a ride. We flew over our house and circled the building where the party was being held. He was so happy to get to do it. He was on the local news that night in a story about his party. He enjoyed watching highlights of the party on television. He laughed and pointed at himself and exclaimed his usual "ME!!!" followed up with the naming of the others at his party. Since then, he has been looking at his helicopter and party pictures and laughing and smiling as he remembers.

Since the party, Zach has made friends with Jodi Foose. They had quite a connection since one of Jodi's sisters also had progeria. I watched the two of them play, and I knew it was like Jodi had found a lost brother. It was great to get to see someone who cared so much for Zachary and understood all he was going through without me having to explain it to her. The first time I watched Zachary and Jodi lay in our living room floor and play together it was obvious they were best friends. What surprised me was how fast they came to know each other. It sometimes takes a while to build up Zachary's trust, but he immediately took up with Jodi. It was apparent Zachary recognized Jodi understood his condition and the fact she could immediately see him for who he was. In turn Zachary treated Jodi like family and the fun began. She often came to visit and when she was there we just let them do their own thing. This was kind of unusual because most of the time Zachary wanted Molly or I to be involved in whatever he was doing. But he was content when spending time with Jodi. Little had to be said between the two of them because it seemed they knew what each other was thinking.

July 28, 2005

The baby they said would not make it to three months is now the kid who is three years old. We are so proud of Zachary's three years.

At our house we have landscaping with many flowers that we plant and grow each season. Zachary enjoys the flowers and helps with the planting and care of them. He loves to hold the water hose and sprinkle the flowers in the evening. He is so proud of the flowers, and we talk about the many colors of blooms we have.

I seem to be more obsessed with the struggling flowers, so much so I can't even enjoy the blooms of all the beautiful ones. Instead, I look and can only see the few flowers that are struggling. I focus my attention on their survival. I even brought home some flowers given to me by the plant nursery because they were wilted due to neglect and surely would not survive should they be planted. I liked the idea of the challenge and, after all, they were free. I planted the flowers in the best spot and then cared for them each day as needed. Many of these flowers eventually produced vibrant blooms, and did I ever enjoy their bounty! I get so much more satisfaction from the challenge these flowers present to me. I could look at our flowerbed filled with blooming flowers of many colors and smile when a guest would give a compliment on the beauty of it. I would then say, "Yeah, but see that one right there with the bright purple blooms? It was practically dead when the nursery gave it to me for free; now look at what it has produced."

August 9, 2005

Zachary went to the "Bullnanza" bull-riding event last weekend. He was able to sit behind the chutes with the bull riders. It was neat getting to lean against the rail and watch them get ready for the ride and then hobble off. He met all the World

Bull-Riding Champions from the last five years. We got to watch the bulls be loaded behind the arena. Zach really liked it. They played loud rock-n-roll music each time a bull and rider came out of the chute for their eight-second ride. From our front-row seats we anticipated the first bull and rider to burst out of the chute. Zachary leaned up to watch between the two metal rails. As the first bull and rider came out of the chute, the crowd cheered, and Zachary lunged forward in an excited attempt to join the bull ride. Luckily, I had a grip on the back of his shirt and caught him before he was able to have his turn at eight-seconds of glory with a bull! Zachary does not lack confidence and the need for adventure.

The Lazy E was the event organizer, and they sure were nice to Zach. They were calling the next day asking if we wanted to come back for that evening's rodeo event. They said all the cowboys were asking about him. The world champion rider told Zach he was going to ride the bull for him that night. He was the last rider, and only eight out of twenty-five had stayed on. I thought it was a bold promise for the cowboy to make. But I guess Matt Austin knew what he was talking about when he looked at Zach and told him he would ride the bull. Zach was pleased to see him stay on the bull and clapped as the eight-second buzzer sounded and then Matt tipped his hat toward Zachary.

August 20, 2005

Last night Molly and I took Zachary and Heidi to Tulsa to see the Veggie Tales show. He has been a big fan since he received a music CD from his aunt Jackie that actually used his name in the songs. We had reserved great seats to assure that Zach would be able to see. It was so exciting to see his expression when the Veggie Tales took to the stage and started singing the songs he already knew. He smiled the entire show, and I held him up so he could see. He clapped and danced the entire time. He would keep pointing things out to Heidi as if trying not to let her miss anything.

August 25, 2005

We are lucky to be living in a time and a place we are able to adequately take care of a child with special needs. I look around and consider things that are critical to provide for him:

- House
- Controlled temperature
- Health care
- Medicine
- School
- A Stay-at-home parent to provide constant care
- A job that allows me to spend time each day with Zach
- Ability to afford items Zach needs

September 8, 2005

I took Zach on his first hunting trip. We went out on a dove hunt together. This was a much-anticipated trip that we had discussed many times before. I got all his things ready and woke him up early before his mom knew what was going on. Once I woke him up, he couldn't wait to get his camouflage clothes on. I told mom we were leaving, and she insisted he was too young to go. I said "maybe so" as we left. First stop was the most critical, the donut shop. He was excited as we entered, and he got to pick out his own donut. He insisted we get some other donuts to take home for the family.

We arrived at the hunting spot and we unloaded Rock, our hunting dog. Zachary gave constant direction to the dog and watched his every move. We walked down the field's edge together with him in my arms. Zach's keen eye surveyed this field and the adjacent one for birds. We made it to a shaded corner, and I set up a folding chair next to some hay bales. I asked him if he wanted to sit in the chair, and he settled right in. He then insisted I put his hat on him, and then, to my surprise, he pointed at my shotgun leaned up against the hay bale several feet away and motioned to put the gun in his lap. He was quite pleased when I obliged him with his request. He looked over the gun in his lap with great pleasure and then began again looking for some birds. He did not see any, so he directed Rock over into the brush to find some birds. Rock followed his order and then Zach insisted he saw some ducks. His imagination was working for him, but he was having fun.

After a while we did see some doves while walking around, but I did not shoot at them, since I had left the shotgun against the hay bale so I could carry Zach in my arms. And that was certainly fine by us, because we were enjoying being together. We saw some crows, cardinals, doves, and squirrels. Before we left I shot my gun to see how Zach would react. After the first shot he just laughed and yelled "Boom!" back at me. With that I shot two more times, and he just smiled. I asked if he was having fun, and he smiled and said "Uh-huh!" with much appreciation.

September 10, 2005

I took Zachary, Courtney, Hobbs, and Rock to the Walk-N-Wag annual fundraiser for the Payne County SPCA. Zachary was so proud to hold Hobbs' leash while I pushed him in the stroller. Because he is sensitive to light, he wore a hat and kept his head down. He doesn't usually like to go out in the middle of the day but this was a time he could show off. We all had a great time walking around the trail. Zachary kept making me stop if he saw ducks in the water so he could say hello.

September 16, 2005

Zachary has been attending school for three weeks. He goes to a three-year-old class two days a week, and Molly and Hobbs go to assist. Zachary is an enthusiastic student. He is always excited to go and never complains. He soaks up every moment at school and has much fun with his new friends and teachers. Every morning he wants to know if this is a school day.

This week he and Molly went class to class with Hobbs to demonstrate how service dogs work. They also took the opportunity to speak to the classes about being kind to special needs children. Zach was shy for the first class, but once he understood how things would go he really started helping out Molly. He held Hobbs' leash and let Hobbs retrieve his pen and take off his socks. Zach is such an exceptional student, and it makes me proud to watch him develop and inspire others.

He has embraced his opportunity to live and experience another set of life's challenges. It would be so easy for him to dislike school and to be discouraged by all the challenges before him. But instead, he just keeps overcoming obstacles and enjoying his existence.

Zachary's teachers are so nice to him. I doubted he would ever be able to attend school without Molly or me with him. But watching him with his teachers, I know he will be able to go to school on his own with his teachers. The school and teachers are very accommodating to him. They make him feel very comfortable and loved. They even adjust the thermostat to his preference!

I never would have imagined school could have worked out so well for Zachary. He is very passionate about his schoolwork. He tells me about his day and shows me his schoolwork when I come home. He takes it very seriously and is proud of what he accomplishes. He is learning new songs and likes to sing them for the family and try to teach us the words and motions. Molly made a CD of all his favorites so we can sing them in the evening. His favorites are: "Going on a Bear Hunt," "Three Green Speckled Frogs," "The Monkey and Alligator Song," and "The Five Little Chicks Went Out to Play." He also enjoys doing the crafts and painting. Our refrigerator looks like an art gallery! Isn't it ironic he enjoys something that is so challenging to him because of his condition? It goes to prove that if you have enough desire, you can accomplish many things despite limitations.

The staff at his school has sure grown fond of him. Their genuine love for our son is apparent in their actions. His teachers adjust the classroom thermostat to a temperature pleasing to

Zachary because he is so hot natured. They too are amazed at how the Boss controls activities. He often decides which class activity will happen next. They comment on how amazing it is for a child so small and with limited mobility to be able to control the activities of a class full of children.

One of the workers for the school district took particular interest in Zachary and volunteered to make him a custom-fit toilet. The typical store-bought training toilets for children his age simply did not fit his body. The worker came out to get the necessary measurements to ensure a custom fit for Zachary. He was no doubt surprised at how small the portable toilet needed to be. The worker took great care in designing and constructing the perfect toilet for Zachary. The toilet was a very soft vinyl covered chair with a stainless steel removable pan beneath it. It was the perfect solution for Zachary's need. Zachary let us know it was quite comfortable, and now the simple task of going to the bathroom would not be such a hassle. We no longer had to hold him so he would not fall into the toilet, allowing Zachary more independence. Often Zachary's bowel movements were difficult and caused much pain for him. I was so thankful to see that this new custom toilet provided Zachary with the proper position, and he was now able to relax and use the bathroom much more easily. The kind gesture of this man taking the time to build Zachary's toilet has increased his quality of life and spared him much pain. All my expectations were exceeded, and I am so thankful for this man providing something to my son that I had not thought of. It means so much to me to know others can be so caring for my son. Tears came to my eyes when I heard the worker commented on how it was an honor to build the toilet for Zachary.

October 26, 2005

Zachary spends so much time with me that he is really starting to act like a parent to his brothers and sisters. When I walk in the house from work, he is usually with me until we go to bed, and I leave for work the next day. So as a result he has figured out just about everything about me. He knows when I walk into Courtney and Derek's rooms I am checking to see if their room is clean, their homework is done, etc. He now inspects their room for me and even gives them orders for me. It is kind of amazing he can assess a room and know what items require picking up and putting away.

He also generally knows what my reaction is going to be for each situation encountered. He knows the bedtimes of his brother and sisters, and if we pass them in the hall he immediately starts barking at them, saying "Bed!" and pointing toward their rooms. He really has parenting figured out or at least he really knows me.

I gave him a quiz the other day and realized he knows everything about our lives. When the family's laundry is piled on the bed to be folded, he can tell who each piece of clothing belongs to. And that is clothing for six people! He knows where every item in the house is kept and when anything is out of place. We were upstairs, and I asked him several questions and he got them all correct. I asked him to point to Heidi's bed, her mattress, her sheet, the stereo, the attic door, the shotgun shells (kept in a small decorative tin), and the sea shells (he knew the difference in types of shells). I could not come up with anything he was not aware of.

He is brilliant for his age and is an exceptional student. Best of all, he does not let his physical pain and ability hold him back from his happiness. I know what his secret is. He gets his happiness from making others happy, doing God's work! He does not hinge his personal happiness to only himself. He relies on satisfying others and God.

Everything he does he keenly watches your reaction. Every move he makes requires much energy and, I suspect, pain too. I have watched him, and most of what he does is for others. That is why he is so interested in your reaction to what he does. He wants to please you. It makes me so proud to say I am pleased with every action Zachary makes. What more could a father want? That is why our family is so happy. No matter what our personal situation may be.

October 29, 2005

The family went on a duck hunt together. Molly, Heidi, Zachary, Derek, Courtney, Grandpa, and I went on the hunt. This was Zachary's and Heidi's much anticipated first duck hunt. Courtney and Derek were experienced and happy to show their little brother and sister how to hunt duck.

They enjoyed every moment of the adventure. They were so excited and curious to hear the shotgun fired. They managed to scare off any ducks that tried to land in the decoys, but that was all right. They had fun exploring the shoreline and getting in and out of the hunting blind.

We hunted until dark, and they were not a bit scared by the darkness. They seemed to feel right at home out there in the wild. The next morning, they were both ready to go back and do it again. However, I don't think Molly had fully recovered from wrestling them around yet. It was great for them to get to experience an activity the older kids often talk about. I think it filled a gap, and they now felt apart of this family activity.

I will never forget Zachary waving at the circling ducks, playing peek-a-boo with his mom in the blind, Heidi blowing the duck call and refusing to let me have it back, and Derek sitting with his shotgun at the corner of the blind waiting for a shot.

October 31, 2005

Zachary has encountered many clowns at circuses and parties. He is very shy and even scared of them. He seems to think they are trying to trick him by wearing a costume and makeup. The harder the clowns try to befriend him, the more Zachary shies away. When faced with a clown Zachary becomes very suspicious and never takes his eye off them. The clowns however refuse to give up. Clowns from all over the country send him letters with photos in the mail every week. He enjoys getting the letters and thinks the photographs are silly but when I ask him if he wants to go see the clowns again he quickly informs me, "No way!"

The standoff with the clowns has gone on for months. They mean so well and try so hard, but Zachary refuses to give in. Much to my surprise, when I asked him what he wanted to dress up as for the "fall party" to be held at his school he responded, "A clown." I could not believe it. Each time I asked, he became more adamant he was going to be a clown. And so a clown he was for the party. His costume had already been decided, so Molly made a quick trip to Wal-Mart last night in hopes of finding a clown costume that would fit him. All she found were toddler sizes, so she pulled out the sewing machine to make a few alterations. He also wanted Heidi to be a clown with him. In contrast, her costume was a little tight. When the news of this hit the clown community, a victory was declared by the clowns. A few weeks later Zachary received via mail his induction into the Clowns of America. He was given the clown name "Okie Dokey" and it couldn't be more fitting. He was very pleased to join the persistent clowns, and I am never ceased to be amazed at Zachary and why he does the things he does.

November 2, 2005

At night when I lock the door before bed, I think about what I am protecting. It is always Zachary who comes to my thoughts. He is special to me. He comes before my possessions and even myself. What are you thinking about protecting when you lock your home's door? Are you protecting what's really important?

Molly cares so much for Zachary that she took him and his service dog, Hobbs, to speak at Zachary's school as well as his older brother and sister's school. Molly explained why special needs children sometimes look different, and in return she found almost all of the children responding with an outpouring of love and interest in Zachary and Hobbs. Not only did Molly do something great for Zachary, she also did something great for every special needs person these children would encounter the rest of their lives. Not understanding and being afraid to accept and love a special needs person is a challenge today's children continue to face. Children deserve an explanation about special needs people and need to be encouraged on treating them with respect and love.

November 7, 2005

Zachary, Hobbs, Molly, Molly's mom, and I attended the 2005 Progeria Research Foundation's scientific workshop on progeria and the Fundraising Gala Event in Boston Massachusetts.

Molly and I were invited to speak in a panel discussion at the workshop. We addressed 95 scientists from nine countries. They were leaders in the fields of genetics, biochemistry, cellular biology, etc. The focus of the workshop was potential treatments for progeroid syndromes. We were specifically asked to present a discussion on what it is like for the patients and families of those who have this condition. It was exciting to have an opportunity to address such experts in this field. It was even more exciting to answer detailed questions and have the scientists acknowledge how much our presentation has helped their research. Perhaps even more exciting was seeing how much we were able to motivate these scientists by explaining our gratitude, expectations, and the impact they have already had on us.

I participated in the entire workshop and was able to obtain answers to many questions I have as both a parent and scientist. It was very emotional for me to be able to observe the scientific presentations and finally understand on a cellular level the effects of progeria. I was able to see the images of the mutations on the Lamin A gene and see the models of the damage done to the body. It was exciting to see this followed by presentations of the effects of experimental treatments curing these progeria-affected cells, also to see the mouse models and other models that are the next step towards a treatment for the patients. In between each presentation I was bombarded with questions about Zachary. It was great to be able to provide direct answers that may somehow help the scientists with their efforts. I was also able to come away with many new friendships with these scientists. It is a comfort to a parent knowing so many brilliant people are working on curing Zachary and the others with progeria syndromes. It was an awesome feeling when I was able to let some of the scientists hold Zachary in their arms. I hope they are able to remember that feeling of holding Zachary, seeing his blue eyes, and experiencing his smile when they are working long hours and overcoming all the challenges that are on the path of finding a cure for progeria.

Here is part of the message I presented at the workshop:

> Maintaining hope is easy when you have a son who gives so much back to you. In spite of his limitations, he is able to accomplish so much and inspire so many. The thing that I become the saddest about when I ponder the thought of losing our son soon due to his prognosis is that he will not be able to continue to inspire his fellow man. A few years ago I was visiting a friend in Hawaii and met his teenage nephew. I was extremely impressed with this teenager's compassion for his friends and the way he was living his life. He seemed perfectly healthy but after being around him for a few days I knew there was something special about him. He was having such a positive impact on me and everyone around him. I felt compelled to ask my friend about his teenage nephew. My friend knew immediately what I was talking about and explained that as a young child his nephew was diagnosed with a terminal disease and was able to overcome this thanks to a cure developed by research scientists and doctors. I had just witnessed the true resulting miracle of all the work the scientists and doctors had accomplished. This child had not been restored to what I consider a "normal" condition. He had been cured and was now living a life that was even better than "normal". That is why I believe a cure for a "few" can impact "everyone". The scientists who cured this child were able to impact my life sixteen years later and I am sure their miraculous work is still carrying on.
>
> I hope a cure will come for Zachary so that I can continue to witness his work here on earth. He has already accomplished so much in 3 years. He works so hard to please and inspire everyone and our hope is that the scientific research will allow him to continue his work for as long as possible.

While I participated in the workshop during the days, Molly, Zachary, and MeMa Sandy were able to get to know Megan Nighbor and her family. The Foundation had made plans for them to attend the Boston Children's Museum and take a tour ride on the Duck Boat around Boston to see the sights. Zachary had a great time and would tell me all about what he was doing during our breaks. His friend Jodi Foose came from Tulsa as well as her mother Terry Foose from California and another long time family friend of the Foose family. In the evenings the Foose family, Megan and her family and us would all get together and hang out in the lobby for hours. Sam Berns, another child with progeria, was able to join us on a few occasions. The kids were so happy to be with other kids just like them!

November 10, 2005

Molly, Zachary, and I attended The Progeria Research Foundation 2005 Gala fundraising event in Boston. The foundation has an award known as the Amy Award to honor the charitable work of individuals. The award is named after Amy Foose, who died from progeria in 1985. Amy is an inspiration to many, and the award honors her memory. One of the most memorable moments of the evening was watching Chip Foose (Amy's brother) receive the Amy Award. He was given this award due to his work for the foundation in raising both awareness and funds. I was impressed at how Chip was still giving to others, even in his moment of recognition. Chip spoke that the reason he was able to help in such a way was because his mother, Terry Foose, had dedicated her life to Amy and made sure Chip and his siblings had a good life. It was very emotional for me to watch as Chip called his mother to the stage and asked her to keep the award at her house for display.

December 5, 2006

Zachary painted a picture for Nelly the elephant, who lives at Hollywood Animals. His teacher, Ms. Lynn, sent the painting to the elephant, and it was hung on Nelly's fence. Nelly is a talented elephant and is known for paintings. The elephant in turn painted a picture using Zachary's favorite colors of purple, green, and yellow. Zachary was very proud when he received the painting in the mail.

January 17, 2006

Zachary and Daddy's quote: "Zach is just like Daddy. The only difference is that Zach's just better!" This quote came to Zachary and I while we were in a hospital room talking about things we had done and were going to do. We both laughed with amusement when I said it.

Zachary is the leader of our family in his special way. I try to live up to his example. I try to maintain an attitude and commitment to serve God to equal Zachary's. This all in spite of the fact Zachary has it tougher than all of us put together.

He has been tested at a young age, and he is passing his test. His condition has allowed him the chance to inspire many others. He has not let God down. Not even once. Zachary is on his way to heaven. That is what I strive for everyday, and I often fail. I have no excuses for my failures. All I can do is understand what God wants for me and my family and live God's way.

January 24, 2006

Zachary passed away yesterday. We can cry for Zachary; however, we ought to be rejoicing in his complete life. Zachary figured out at a young age his purpose. His purpose was to serve God. With that everything else fell into place. That is our sole purpose.

We can spend years trying to figure this out, or get around this fact, or attempt to find satisfaction through earthly possessions. But once we finally figure it out, then and only then are we satisfied and is God satisfied with us. Zachary seems to have done this from day one through his final day here on earth. As a father, there is no more I could hope for in a son to accomplish. Zachary has fulfilled his purpose and has accomplished his mission.

Let us realize through Zachary's life that we are all on the same mission. When we are weak, doubting, or asking for answers to life's questions, remember Zachary and his life he led for us all to witness.

January 25, 2006

One of Zachary's favorite things to do was "roll call," in which he went down a list and named those he loves. He would lie next to Molly and me and list the names or give his approval while we listed the names. It might be a birthday party list, a list of family members, a list of friends, a list of those who visited him, or a list of those who called or sent him letters.

Zachary was constantly concerned for those he knew and loved. He wanted to know where they were at all times, especially before he went to sleep at night.

I know Zachary is now in heaven doing his roll call once again. Zachary wanted to please everybody all the time. I pray that we all can make him happy now and answer his roll call at the gates of heaven.

Part III

Reflections

The following is a journal titled "Reflections." It captures the events and feelings I experienced in the first weeks after Zachary's death.

Destination Arrived

A few weeks before Zachary passed away, I began writing a story about him entitled "Destination Arrived!" I started by stating, "Zachary has achieved what far too few of us have. He has arrived at his destination." I had planned on continuing the story by telling of Zachary's good work and faith. That is as far as I got in writing it when Zachary became very sick and we went to the hospital, where he spent his final ten days here on earth. Now looking back at what I had written in that beginning sentence, it amazes me how revealing a look into Zachary's life this introduction was. It is inspirational to me to see that I felt Zachary had arrived at his destination in life, unknowingly to me at the time, just prior to his death. It is as if he completed his mission. When I wrote this, Zachary was not feeling sick, and we were actively working on a clinical trial for him to potentially be cured of his condition. When I began writing the story "Destination Arrived" I never would have guessed the story would only need to be one sentence in length. But I guess that is similar to Zachary's life, short yet accomplished and complete.

Final Moments

During Zachary's final moments, Molly told him, "If you see Jesus, go with Him. Don't be afraid. We love you and will see you again soon." That is when Molly completed her mission as Zachary's mother. She accomplished all she could for Zachary, and now we could see Jesus was calling Zachary home.

As difficult as it was at that moment to tell Zachary those words and let go of him, it was what God wanted. Molly and I will spend the rest of our lives continuing to struggle between our human nature of wanting to keep our son with us always and understanding he ultimately was and is God's son. I am doubtful we will ever overcome our human nature of wanting our son with us while we are living our life on earth. We can only compensate those feelings with knowing Zachary is now with his almighty Father, and we will soon enough join him.

On Zachary's final day of his life he stared into my eyes as I have never been looked at before. It was clear he was letting me know what his explicit wishes were. At the time, I did not know they were his final wishes. He was hungry and wanted to eat dinner. Lying in a hospital bed, he was hooked up to oxygen, and we were being very careful about food intake. We did not want him to choke. But when Zachary looked at me, it was clear he was commanding me to give him his dinner. Per his special request, Molly went and bought him a spaghetti dinner. When she entered the room Zachary looked up and said loudly, clearly, and cheerfully, "Hi!" to his mom. This would be his last dinner. Thankfully that final dinner did not make him sick or present difficulties for him. We smiled as he sucked in the noodles as I fed him.

These two events, Zachary looking deep into my eyes and Zachary greeting Molly as she brought him dinner, were our final two earthly high points with our son. This would be the last time Zachary would "boss" us. How we enjoyed being bossed by the Boss. We will never forget how happy Zachary was when I answered him and said he could have his dinner and how he exclaimed his joyful greeting when Molly came back to him with his dinner.

That evening Zachary was bossing around his nurses by asking for a drink and letting them know it was time for medicine. How he kept up with his medicine schedule is beyond me. I do know he sure enjoyed being in control of the medical team by reminding them of their duties. He was so satisfied when they thanked him for the timely reminders. His teacher and principal visited him, and he sang one last school song and played with the finger puppets. The song was one of his favorites, the Frog Song. Aunt Jackie and Cousin Jamie visited him, and he showed them he was as brave as ever. Our friend Carmen had just arrived to help Molly and me with Zachary. Zachary was showing improvement and was in good spirits. Molly and I were strategizing on the best care for him after reviewing his latest laboratory test results. We agreed on an immediate care plan and went through our checklist to make sure we were doing all we could for him. We were trying so hard to make him healthy enough to go home again.

Molly and I lied in the hospital bed with him and loved on him. We were doing his favorite thing, showering him with our affection. Suddenly, I noticed Zachary was struggling to breathe, and I immediately called upon all the medical resources to save him. Zachary did not say anything, but I could sense how serious the situation was. The next hour would be Zachary's last with us. Molly and I were there to help and be with him during his final fight for life, and we know Zachary never gave up; he was simply called unto heaven.

I held Zachary's hand and helped the medical team try to save him in his final moments. He then clinched my hand and I knew he was gone. I'll never forget what the last surge of strength from Zachary felt like. With it he said goodbye for now to me. We tried three more times to revive him, and fifteen minutes later the doctors said that was it. I composed myself and thanked the dozen or more medical staff that were in the room trying to save Zachary. We spent the next couple of hours saying goodbye to Zachary's earthly body.

Molly and I had to make medical decisions for him many times. Now we question every decision and wonder if different choices would have resulted differently. We decided not to put him on a ventilator while he was still talking to us and showing signs of improvement. We were informed he would be difficult to place on a ventilator and there would be high risks in doing so. We finally decided we would rather live with the decision of not going on a ventilator while Zachary was still very responsive rather than going on a ventilator with Zachary in a forced comatose state. It all came down to risks, and we had little with which to compare since progeria is so rare and unusual. All involved agreed putting Zachary in a comatose state and on a ventilator would be extremely risky, and he would likely not survive the process. So we decided to put this off to use as a last resort. Now we are forced to live with all our decisions we made for Zachary. In the end, the ventilator did not work for Zachary, and there is no clear option in hindsight that would have worked. Still we question all our decisions and wonder if there was something else we should have done for him. That is the parent in us and I guess those thoughts are unavoidable.

When Zachary passed away, I picked his body up to carry it around the way I had so many times before. It was evident to me Zachary was gone from his body. His forehead became colder and colder each time I kissed it until all remnants of human life were gone. As I walked I held his body against my chest for a couple of hours and reflected on his accomplishments. This time was truly only a reflection of Zachary, and I know he was watching from heaven now. I am completely pleased with his life and know I must move on and continue my life to please God. However, I will always be humbled by the small three-year old Zachary Moore.

Now I drive to work and I have all these thoughts about Zachary, no different than when he was here on earth. As I drive eastward on my way to work, I see the sky as it brightens with anticipation of a sunrise, and I feel Zachary with me. I know he is better off now than he has ever been. As the eastern sky turns brilliant with the light of another day, it is clear; I must do my part to ensure that I, too, will achieve what Zachary has achieved, to be with our true Father in heaven.

Without Zachary

◆ ◆ ◆

I am confident in my faith in God and I accept and understand why Zachary has passed away. I was sad as I lost him, but I was happy he was now in heaven. I knew he was pure and that his home is now in heaven. A home much better than I ever could provide and one he truly deserves. I guess the next logical issue to consume my mind is this feeling of what his death means to me. Furthermore, the parent in me is still working and I keep asking myself, "What could I now do to help Zachary"? What would he want from me? The answer is clear and it tied in with all these thoughts. I too need to ensure that I am living my life for God.

Zachary and I were as close as two people can be. He was my son whom I poured all my efforts, prayers, and hope into. I felt as much responsibility for Zachary's well being as I did my own. At first consideration you may think that most parents feel that way about their child. What I am talking about goes beyond the normal parent-child relationship. Remember, because of Zachary having progeria, I was constantly responsible for his every move. I can give you an example. If he was sitting in a chair I watched him like a hawk to make sure he did not fall and seriously injure himself, as he ate I sat by his side to make sure he did not choke, if he wanted to move across the room I was there to move him, I slept by his side each night to provide the frequent care he needed, I researched the best care for him, and I constantly sought out a cure for him. Many of these tasks were not so much out of necessity but rather out of wanting him to be able to do and enjoy his life. Molly was doing the same for him and we often split all the tasks in order to accomplish them. Zachary and I frequently knew what each other were thinking and my favorite task in life was doing for him all the things that he was physically unable to do because of his condition. Those who saw Zachary and I interact often commented on our special connection. He consumed my thoughts, feelings, admiration, respect, and brought me great joy. God blessed me with so much in Zachary and I give God the ultimate glory for giving him to me as my son. In many ways my success and happiness were all tied to Zachary. As long as he was with me and I was providing for him I was doing right. Our immediate complex situation due to his health ultimately gave my life spiritual simplicity. As difficult as the situation was, it still brought me much happiness to be with him.

When he died in my arms it was though I died with him. I could then somehow feel and realize my impending judgment and was forced to ask myself how I would fare. This coupled with the fact I no longer had Zachary with me to provide that spiritual simplicity in my life was a sobering reality. This all hit me within minutes of his death. Zachary's death was so personally perceived to me it opened my eyes to the harsh reality of the judgment ahead of me. So much so that I felt like I had a second chance to make sure I get things right. Or at least I now had a more vivid understanding of the true consequences of death in which we all will face.

The bible tells us that at the judgment there will be many with much regret. Only then will they realize it is too late to repent and be saved and they will then understand the meaning of eternity. They will be cast down and forever separated from God. This will be a moment when all truth can no longer be denied. I pray that as you read this you too will consider your own life and make or reaffirm the decision to live for God.

Zachary's not here this morning to drink the milk foam from the top of my latté. There does not seem to be much of a reason to get out of bed. I remember there used to be a dispute on weekend mornings at our house to see who the lucky one was to go get

Zachary out of bed. Since he was unable to walk, he relied on the family to get him out of bed in the mornings. He would usually yell out for someone to hear he was awake, and then his brother and sisters would ask me if they could be the one to go get Zachary. His sister Courtney most liked going and getting him out of bed. She always dropped whatever she was doing to be with Zachary. I seldom let them go get him without me, because I wanted to be there for him too. It was such a precious moment when he would see your face and you his. He would yell out or say something clever.

He greeted each day with great anticipation. For him, the joy of each day seemed centered around spending time with his family and friends. Zachary truly awoke each morning with an attitude you would expect from a child on Christmas morning, or their birthday, or their first day of a vacation you had been planning for weeks.

He would typically start his day by doing a roll call to see where everyone was. Naturally, Heidi was always the most important on the roll call list, because she was the baby. Zachary also immediately asked for his service dog, Hobbs. It was instant motivation in the morning for me to hear and see Zachary. The mornings I left for work, I would peek in on him sleeping and pray for him before I left.

As I look at photographs of Zachary taken two months ago, it does not seem possible he is now gone. It is difficult for the mind of a parent to accept such a loss. Although Zachary had obvious health problems, he was so full of life, even just weeks before his death. It does not quite seem real to me he is gone. Somehow I keep expecting to see him when I come home from work or walk into his bedroom. Yesterday, Heidi and I were playing in the kitchen together when we heard the familiar sound of the electric toy car Zachary used to ride around in. Both of us instantly stopped what we were doing; I thought Zachary was driving the car, and Heidi yelled out "Zachary!" Just for a second, my mind tricked me into thinking Zachary was right there in the next room. Heidi wanted him to be there so much she insisted I carry her into the room where, to her disappointment, she determined it was Derek moving the car.

Yes, we all miss Zachary, and at times it is hard to accept he is really gone. Heidi asks about Zachary many times each day. We can only tell her Zachary has gone on to heaven. I will focus my efforts on joining Zachary in heaven. I will focus on my relationship with Molly and raising Heidi, Courtney, Derek, and Lindsay so they too will go to heaven.

Molly and I realize in our grief that things will never be as good as they were when Zachary was with us. We certainly reached a pinnacle of greatness in our lives with Zachary, and I feel such a high point is not possible with Zachary gone. If you are thirsty, is one swallow of water better than two? Although things will never be as good as they once were, they can still be good enough to be happy and satisfied. If not, we will never be able to carry on. *It is all right if things are not as good as they once were.* Things can still be good; it just may be in a different way. Understanding and accepting that is the biggest part in recovering from our loss.

We struggle with emotions: Could we have made better decisions? Zachary was so strong to the end. Could we have done something different or better? Would we have rather seen him give up or would we be happier knowing he fought to the end? Zachary did fight to the end. Even in final respiratory distress, he was doing what we asked of him to get better. The last hour of his pain is so hard to get out of our heads. All I could tell Molly as she relives those minutes of pain is that it was better being there for him than not knowing what occurred in the room during his final moments. At least it was for Molly and I. But such images damage your heart forever.

Life without Zachary presents basic challenges. Now I don't even know what to wear in the morning. I used to dress according to what Zachary and I were going to be doing that particular day. Each day with Zachary was full of activities. We were always able to make our own fun. Making your own fun is a special connection I wish all families could experience.

My new fear is being faithful now that the leader we had in Zachary is gone. We try to remind ourselves he is only gone in the flesh and not in spirit. More importantly, God is always here to lead us. Molly told me she cannot imagine living another fifty years without Zachary. I let her know if it does take fifty years, in the end it will all seem short, and in comparison to eternity, fifty years isn't long at all. The focus is now on doing what it takes to make it to heaven. Eternity is what we need to be concerned about.

Molly reminded me that we treated Zachary like he deserved to be treated when he was here. Everyone tells us what great parents we were to him. It is hard for us to accept this praise now. We were only doing what was right, and Zachary gave so much in return. We were so very proud of him, and now it's our turn to make him proud of us. We will do this by doing God's work, for that is what Zachary always wanted. Zachary cared so much for everyone around him. To care so much for another when your own problems are in fact insurmountable was one of Zachary's inspiring qualities.

Heidi and I were asked by a friend how she was doing. We told them she was doing well. Our friend said to Heidi that Zachary's now in heaven. Heidi understands because she immediately asked for Zachary's book *Picture Me with Jesus*. This was a book with pictures of Zachary cut and pasted to be with Jesus in the pages of the book. I knew then she understood, even at the age of two. Heidi insists Zachary has been sent back to heaven.

As I sit in my office back at work, I'm surrounded by photographs of Zachary. I hesitate to look at his photograph, but I can't focus on his face. No matter how hard I try, the photograph does not represent a clear enough image of his face to satisfy my desire to see him. I blink and shake my head but it does not help. Nothing will ever be the same.

I telephone home to Molly, and I ask her how she is doing. In our conversation I find myself wanting to ask her to put "Boss" on the phone. I keep this thought to myself because I don't want to further upset her. She pauses in our conversation and I know she is having the same thoughts of handing the phone to Zachary and seeing him smile, hearing him say "Daddy," and he then telling me what the two of them are doing that day. But Zachary is not there to talk with now. Instead I ask about Heidi, and Molly asks me how Courtney and Derek were doing when I dropped them off at school. How lucky Molly and I are to have the kids and each other. How lucky we are to have our faith.

A major emotional struggle I now have is facing the fact I am no longer taking care of Zachary. He is out of my control. I have no say in what goes on with him. Even though I know he is in God's permanent care now, it is difficult for me to let go of physically caring for him.

There are many reasons for this struggle: caring for him was rewarding, it was my primary focus for 3½ years, and it brought so much enjoyment to my days. I feel out of control or even helpless now. All things seem pointless or at least not as important as they once were.

If I embrace a sense of relief in knowing Zachary is now with God and I no longer need worry about him, I, in turn, feel guilty as a parent. I cannot let go of worrying and caring about Zachary. As parents we are programmed to not let go so easily. Surely such a strong bond could not be instantaneously broken without any signs of the loss. If a lake dries up, would you not be able to see the lakebed and remnants of the water? Even many years later, after grass and forest have grown over the lakebed, you would still discover the past presence of the lake if you looked close enough or dug beneath the surface.

My emotions are pulled in every direction. If I try to think about Zachary and remember him, I become sad that I cannot be with him. If I try to not think about Zachary and focus on my other children or a new life without Zachary, feelings of guilt take over, stealing the joy from my life. There must be a balance for me.

Zachary was once very dependent on me. Now he is not, just like the first time I saw him in his classroom at school, when I was so surprised to walk in and see him so happy on his own. It was the first time he did not come to me or I to him when we made initial eye contact. Instead, he looked up at me and smiled to let me know he was fine on his own. He was content to be with his teachers and classmates, doing his school activities. He smiled proudly at me to let me know he wanted me to watch him.

Molly is struggling with the loss of Zachary. She feels she has no direction. She receives letters and emails from people letting her know God is with her and they are praying for her. However, she feels lost and without a purpose as a result of Zachary's death. She questioned me about what she should be doing and how much is enough. Last night she prayed to God for a sense of direction. She was distraught and my words of help were unfortunately insufficient.

She went to the bookstore late in the evening to see if she could find some books on finding her direction or perhaps guides for studying the Bible to assist her. She was desperately looking for an answer. Just before going into the bookstore, Molly paused in the parking lot and prayed to God for direction in her life. While at the bookstore she noticed a man watching her and Zachary's service dog, Hobbs, from the end of the aisle. The man finally approached her and started asking questions about the service dog. He asked who the dog was for and when Molly explained it was for her son who had passed away the man asked, "Are you Zachary's mom?" Molly replied, "Yes." The man asked, "You mean you are Zachary Moore's mom?" Molly again smiled and assured him she indeed was. After a long conversation about Zachary and his good works, the man asked Molly to autograph his coffee mug. He then let her know Zachary had "done it again." Molly asked, "What do you mean?" The man replied Zachary had changed another life for the better. He let her know he was inspired after hearing Zachary's stories from Molly, and he was now a changed man.

And just like that, Molly had her answers from God she had asked for two hours earlier in the parking lot of the bookstore. She now understood a purpose still exists for her. She knew in her heart that even without Zachary she could still do sufficient work to please God. Zachary left behind a service dog and a mother that would continue his work on earth.

We need to continually ask ourselves, are we doing enough to satisfy God? If we are called to our judgment, will we be able to please God? Evaluate your own life, look into your heart, seek out opportunities to please God, and then you will be on the righteous path.

Zachary received numerous letters from prison inmates. They wrote to him because they had seen him on television or read about him in the newspaper. The letters came from criminals doing long-term sentences for serious crimes. They wrote to Zachary to let him know how much his story had inspired them. They told of how they were overwhelmed with emotions when they saw how happy Zachary was and how hard he tried even with his severe challenges. Many prisoners had a photograph of Zachary on their cell wall. This was special because each prisoner is only allowed four photographs on their wall. In their choice of a photograph of Zachary, who they did not even know in person, it was obvious he was again inspiring individuals in desperate situations without even being there in person. Just the news of his story was enough to give hope to these prisoners. That is the power of living righteously.

Now as I look at a photograph of Zachary on my desk I say to myself, "There is the Boss." I long to lay my hands upon him but realize I will no longer touch him in this life. I reflect on how so many times before I did lay my hands on him to comfort him, massage him, and kiss him over and over again. I recall lying with him in the floor at home and kissing his head and focusing so hard on how it felt to be with him, because I knew there was a strong chance I would be without him later. The affection I showed Zachary by kissing him on the head would last for minutes. These were some of the few moments he sat still and just let me shower him with affection and attention. Any other time he was counteracting my attention with his playful commands that earned him the name of the Boss.

And now here I am without him. While I long for him, I do not have any regrets in the quality of life we provided for him and the amount of love we gave him. The only catch is that as his father I could never have done enough to satisfy my love for him as my son. I would trade or do anything for another moment with him. I will not be consumed with thoughts of what I did not do or thoughts of what could have happened if his life had been extended. The best I could have accomplished was having no regrets, however, not complete satisfaction in my time with him. Now I will wait until I am in heaven before I have complete satisfaction. That is what I am working for now.

I can't help but pause in the doorway of Zachary's room at our house. I remember listening in the dark for him to be breathing to make sure he was all right prior to leaving for work. Now when I listen it is silent. If it were not for my faith, how could I explain or accept Zachary being gone? Through my faith I rejoice in knowing he is in the care of his Savior forever.

The drive to work on a Monday morning is a tough one these days. It is a late winter day, and I drive by the ponds and lakes and on them see the ducks that Zachary and I will never get to hunt together the way we often talked about. I am thankful we did get to hunt together, if only a few times. I am even more thankful we had all the fun there was to be had while he was alive and did all the Lord's work there was for us. These thoughts are what help me through another week without Zachary. He was a good kid and everybody misses him. Heidi still asks about him each day. Her youth allows her to be open and honest about her feelings for Zachary. She will suddenly say, "I miss Zachary." I get much pleasure from watching the acquired traits my kids have as a result of their time with Zachary.

I saw Zachary's cake pan today. This was a cake pan we kept in the lower kitchen cabinet. Heidi was opening the cabinet and I looked and there it was. I immediately thought of what Zachary's reaction would have been. He would have been in my arms and immediately bucked with a surprised expression on his face, pointed, and yelled out "Cake!" so I would be sure and be just as excited as he was. He did this every time we discovered this cake pan.

Many times he would lead me into the kitchen and make me open the cabinet so we could discover the cake pan. He liked this cake pan so much because it represented birthday parties for us all; cooking with mom, grandma, or daddy; and just the simple enjoyment of eating cake.

It has been a couple of weeks now since Zachary passed away. I wonder if every time I see a cake pan I will think of Zachary and how much enjoyment he got out of seeing a cake pan. I don't mind if I do, because I just can't help but smile when I remember that it was very important to him that I be just as excited about the cake pan as he was.

It amazes me how I can vividly remember the handful of times I had to be stern or discipline Zachary. Now he is gone, and I wonder if I was too hard on him. But then I remember how happy he always was, how much respect he had for Molly and me, and he did not act spoiled even though we spoiled him.

I can't help but second-guess the care and decisions I made for Zachary. I ask myself, what if I had done just one little thing differently; would he still be alive today? To obtain some sort of peace of mind, I must accept whatever care or decisions I made because they were always my best attempt to provide for Zachary. This statement would also have to apply to a tragic situation in which a family made a mistake costing their child's life. An example would be a car wreck or other unexpected accident. Still I struggle each day with feelings I somehow let him down. My outlet is to turn to my other family and provide the best care for them. Still I am haunted by these feelings.

I must remember that no person is perfect and free of mistakes. God does not expect perfection and that is why he sent Jesus to save us all. I must make the most of my time remaining to please God. I will do this by staying busy doing His work. Not falling into depression or an unproductive state of mentality. By doing God's work I will be able to continue with my life, though not without missing Zachary.

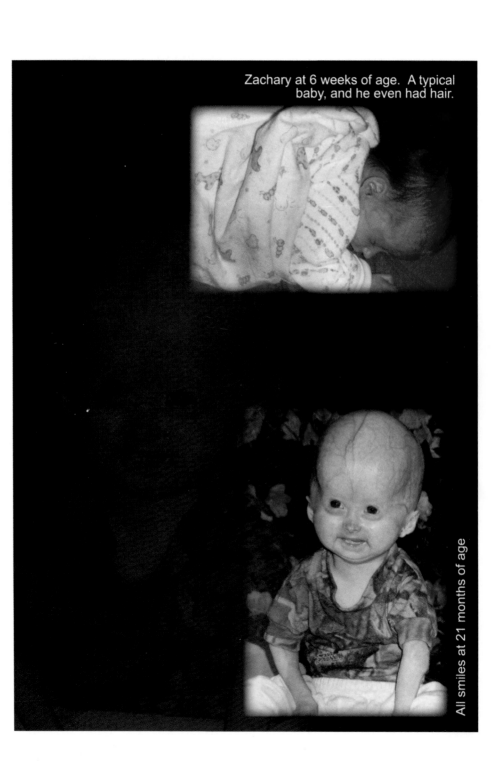

Zachary at 6 weeks of age. A typical baby, and he even had hair.

All smiles at 21 months of age

Exploring the yard with Dad

Age 1, playing with Grandma

The first time he touched his new
baby sister Heidi, January 2004

Helping change baby sister's diaper

On the go with Mom and Heidi

One of his happiest moments as we anticipated a "night on the town" during a family vacation

Zachary cuddling with sister Heidi

Time for prayer

Riding toy horses, Zachary
is 18 months older then Heidi

Wrestling match with his little sister

Camping out in the backyard
with his sister Courtney

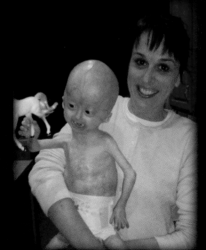

Teasing his mom at 3 years
and 5 months of age

Zachary with all his sisters
and his brother at the zoo

Playing the "bull rider" with
his brother and sister

Zachary and Dad with our friend Megan after the
Progeria Research Foundation's workshop
in Boston, Massachusetts, November 2005

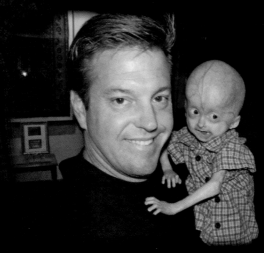

Our friend Chip Foose, leading car design expert from
the hit television show "Overhaulin"

Having fun with his service-dog Hobbs

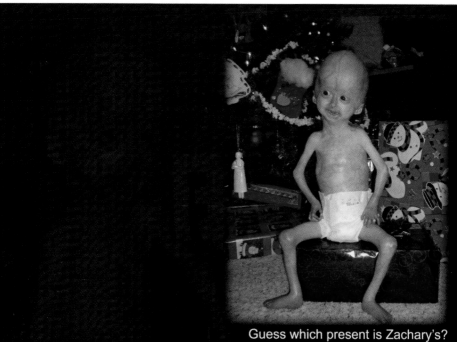

Guess which present is Zachary's?
December 2005

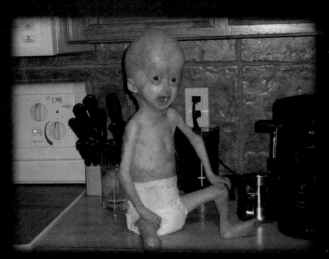

Making a cafe latte for Daddy at 3 years old

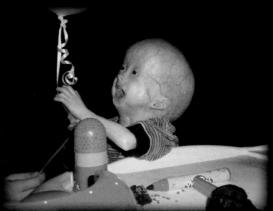

Party time!

Zach's first week with his service-dog Hobbs

Enjoying some cheese after
a day of fishing at the lake

Zachary with his service-dog Hobbs at 24 months of age

Bowling with Dad

Performing the "Going on a Bear Hunt" song with Mom

Zachary at 15 months

Zachary's preferred means of
mobility (Dad's helping hand)

A Christmas picture at school with
Hobbs, December 2005

Zachary and his little sister, Christmas 2005

Honorary Lieutenant Zachary
Moore posing in his uniform

Zachary ready for a day of fishing on the lake

Throwing sugar packets at restaurant, November 2005

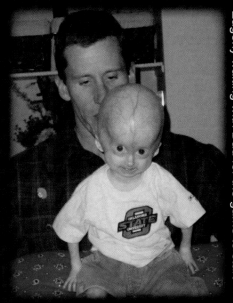

Eagerly waiting with Dad for the game to start

Zachary and Hobbs taking a nap

Being silly with best friend Jodi Foose

Zachary giving Santa his list at the
Make-A-Wish Foundation Christmas party

Zachary draws a car design for Chip
Foose as friend Sam Berns watches

Hanging out with members of the Oklahoma State
University basketball team (left to right: Byron Eaton,
Terrell Harris, Kenny Cooper, David Monds
JamesOn Curry, and Aaron Pettway)

Proud to be at school, September 2005

Working at the Oklahoma County
Sheriff's Office for fun

Driving his new power wheelchair
2 weeks prior to his death

Zachary with his aunt Jackie on
vacation at Silver Dollar City
in Branson, Missouri.

Our family with Jodi Foose (top right) at Zachary's
third birthday party. This was a fundraiser for
the Progeria Research Foundation.

Fundraising with Scott Berns, Chairman
of the Progeria Research Foundation

Clarity

◆ ◆ ◆

I think about how I had Zachary with me and everything was great. Now he is not with me, and he is gone from this earth forever. My mind wants to think it is not fair, it is tragic, how can I go on, or what should I do now? Then I realize the length of life for us all is uncertain. The quicker we realize death is ahead of us all, the better off we will be in deciding on our actions.

There is a moment of clarity when you realize you are not here forever and you will eventually be judged for our works. During that moment of clarity, you come up with all these plans of what to do and what not to do with your life. The plans are often different than what is actually occurring in your life. During the moment of clarity, you decide what is right to do, and then you move on. As you move on away from your moment of clarity that showed you righteousness, it is easy to not do what you decided to do. We often fall back into an unproductive life in the eyes of God.

It is difficult for my mind to continually accept the fact my days are numbered and I will indeed be judged for my work. To help with my focus, I made a written list of things important to my staying righteous. We each need to do whatever we can do to keep us on the path of righteousness. Maybe it is simplifying your life, making a list, surrounding yourself with positive influences, eliminating the unrighteous aspects of life, etc.—whatever works for you personally.

I look at Zachary's photograph on my desk, and I cannot help but see the sad reality that he is gone. What encourages me is the knowledge that he has merely "gone on." He has left this world ahead of me, and it is normal to miss a loved one should they for any reason leave you behind. I am encouraged to know one day I will rejoin him again. When I do, the situation will be perfect and for eternity, and will not consist of disease and other worries. I am motivated, because Jesus has provided me with what it takes to rejoin my son. I will not fall into perpetual depression and become nonproductive in my righteous works. Instead, I will do the work God asks me to do. I desire to be confident when my judgment occurs knowing my acts will be pleasing to God.

If I had to describe what it feels like when your son dies at age three, it would be like this: You know the feeling you get when you become a parent? I describe it as the feelings of love and a strong desire to provide for your child. Your child becomes your life's priority. You know you would do anything and face any challenge for your child. Your instincts take over and you are willing to fight and even lay down your life for your child's well being. Your child is a part of you.

Suddenly, your child dies in your arms, and now you feel a part of you has died with your child. All those dominant parental feelings are instantly not needed, but they remain, leaving your mind and body empty and confused.

I suppose the feeling may be similar to being told by your doctor you have only two weeks to live. Death becomes very real and near to you. You now feel like you are on your way out of this life. That is the way I feel now that my son, who was a part of me, has died. Never again will I feel content in this life. A part of me is gone, and it was the best part.

With all this grief come advantages, though. I am closer to God more now than ever. With death feeling so close, it pushes me to live the life God wants for me. It is a high price to pay for a wake-up call that I should have never needed. I guess that may be why life is challenging and even tragic at times for us all.

More than Sibling Love

♦ ♦ ♦

I remember the day we brought Heidi home from the hospital, five days after her birth. Zachary was waiting in anticipation of his new baby sister. He had spent the past months touching and talking about Molly's tummy and the pregnancy. We explained to him that her tummy was so large because Molly had a baby in it. Zachary sure managed to twist things around and explained to everyone it was his baby in Molly's tummy. He staked his claim on this baby and became insistent it was his should anyone suggest it was Molly's baby or even "our" baby. He maintained this claim and when we brought Heidi home Zachary immediately started calling her *his* baby.

I remember when he was sitting in Molly's lap and I laid Heidi in their lap. Zachary reached down and touched Heidi's face for the first time with such love and compassion. He took Heidi on as his responsibility. He watched her every move and told her how to do everything. He was always so concerned for her and was the first to hear her cry when she woke up from a nap. He would then insist on going and getting her out of her crib. You could not even attempt to leave him behind to get Heidi. I always found it interesting how Zachary claimed Heidi as his baby. I guess I figured it was kind of cool, since he would probably never be a parent himself. This was his chance, and he took it.

We were all playing one evening when Zachary insisted Heidi had something in her mouth that she could choke on. I looked at her, and it did not appear she did, so I quickly dismissed

Zachary's concerns. He kept pointing at her and me and yelling that Heidi had something in her mouth. He knew this was not safe and was very concerned for her. I then checked her mouth and still could not find anything. I told Zachary it was okay and not to worry. I figured that with four of us in the room surely one of us would have noticed what Zachary had noticed. He then became very agitated with me and insisted I do something. I have the utmost respect for Zachary, and I agreed to satisfy him. I took my finger and swabbed out Heidi's mouth and much to my amazement a small sharp-edged toy appeared, and she immediately tried to swallow it. I was able to remove the object before it lodged in her throat. I recall how satisfied Zachary was at the conclusion of the incident as he looked at me. Without saying a word his eyes told me, "I told you so!"

I am very proud of how Zachary's brother and sisters treated him. Never once did they complain about not being able to do something because Molly and I were busy caring for Zachary. They completely understood the time Molly and I dedicated to caring for Zachary. My children understood that although there were many things we were unable to do because of limitations placed on our family due to Zachary's health, there were also many opportunities occurring for us because of Zachary. They too embraced this special child and were always able to extract all the good things he brought to us. There is no doubt that having Zachary improved our family's happiness and brought us closer together than we ever thought possible.

The times when Molly and I were away for weeks caring for Zachary in the hospital our other children did not complain about the situation. Instead, they were only concerned about Zachary's well being. Molly and I made a point to include our children in caring for Zachary. We chose not to isolate them from the reality of Zachary's condition. We explained to them why we were required to provide so much care to him and how that would leave less time for us to care for them. We told them we needed their help too if we were going to succeed in providing for Zachary. They all understood and helped us take great care of Zachary. Zachary was very aware of how much they loved him, and in turn he loved them with all his heart. Our children all understood how special Zachary was, and they too witnessed the gift he brought our family.

Lindsay, Courtney, and Derek all agree the thing they liked most of Zachary was his sense of humor. He loved making them laugh by teasing and playing with them all. Courtney recalls how Zachary would drive his power wheelchair into her room without her knowing and take one of her prized possessions. Only later to reveal it to her and then dash off in his wheelchair with it while he erupted in laughter. Courtney was very touched and say's she will never forget how Zachary would make school projects to give to her. While most kids were making projects for their parents, Zachary cared enough to create art work at school to give to his sister. The teachers gave him the choice of who to make things for and he often considered her. Courtney says her most cherished memory with Zachary was the times they went fishing together.

They all three carry with them photographs of their brother on the cover of their school folders. They are proud of their brother and willing to share him with the world. I asked our kids what the biggest thing was they learned from their brother Zachary and they replied "he taught us kindness". I was even more amazed when I asked Derek to describe Zachary with one word and he replied "helpful". They didn't view their brother as a hindrance or a sad situation. They too chose to see the opportunity and strength it brought our family. This is love in its purest "childlike" form. This is the way God intends us to love each other.

There is no doubt Zachary has shaped their lives and I feel Zachary has accomplished more in preparing our other children for life than even Molly and I can as parents. It seems apparent that Zachary's purpose of surviving an extra 6 months between his two severe cases of pneumonia was to be with Heidi as she became a toddler and so much of her mental development occurred. That is vividly clear now as I am able to observe how much Zachary influenced Heidi. It is now so evident in her personality.

I came in the house from work yesterday, and Heidi yelled out "Daddy!" She learned this from Zachary. Hearing Heidi exclaim my name made me miss him so much. More importantly, it made me so proud of her for two reasons, because she had learned and carried on a wonderful trait from her brother, and because she feels the same about me as Zachary did.

The Mockingbird

---◆◆◆---

Things are not any tougher now that Zachary's gone. I cried, worried, and stressed over his health issues when he was here. The difference is that now it is not compensated for by the enjoyment of being with him.

There is a mockingbird that perches on our backyard fence and looks over the yard. Zachary watched the bird almost daily since early fall. I would not have guessed this bird would have out-lived my son, for birds' lives are so short and fragile when compared to those of humans.

I stare at this bird again this evening as he sits on the fence. I feel disappointed to not have Zachary with me now. I think about how he was changing and improving so much his last three weeks with the use of his new power wheelchair. Seemed like a strange time to lose him. I wonder how many more days the mockingbird will appear on our backyard fence? Sometimes I see that mockingbird and I want to run at him screaming to chase him away so I don't have to face him. Other times I consider him a friendly reminder of one of the many things Zachary enjoyed and we shared together.

It doesn't seem fair—Zachary tried so hard all the time and yet his life ended so soon. He always tried harder than anyone I knew to be healthy, happy, make others laugh, have fun, fit in, make things his own, be like his dad, and please everybody he was acquainted with. Though it may not seem fair, these qualities are what made Zachary better than me and able to do such special work.

I think I may now understand why there are old people who you meet and you look at them and listen to them and assume they have not done much or been many places in their life. They simply talk about kids, family stories, etc. Then something slips out about the fact that they were once in a combat war zone, flew air missions, traveled the world as a performer in a circus, worked exciting and/or dangerous jobs, or worked on amazing projects. This makes me realize what is now important to them as they "reflect" on their lives. They can only now focus on what is really important—things like family, friends, and time spent together—now that they are further down the road in their walk.

I think Zachary was the greatest and most precious thing. I would do absolutely anything for him. I shaped my life around him. I was pleased to consume my mind with thoughts of him. He was the best thing on earth. Do I feel more strongly about Jesus? Yes, and I should. As great as Zachary was, he was that great because of and through Jesus.

Isn't it great that I can feel so strongly about my son and still know Jesus is even greater, the greatest, and He will care for all of us? My son is now with Jesus and that is what compensates for missing him.

On The Progeria Research Foundation website there is a list of children who passed away since 1999 due to progeria. It is titled "in memory of." I look at the list just to see Zachary's name and the others. I recall previously looking at the list and wondering if we would be able to keep his name off the list by curing him. Zachary's name is currently the last one added to the list. I periodically log on to the website and wonder if his name is still the last one added to the list. Wouldn't it be great if no other names would be added to the list and we could find a cure for the other kids with progeria and the future cases? It hurts to know we did not cure Zachary, and I pray no other names will be added to the list through the work of the Lord through science.

Zachary Made
Me Laugh

◆ ◆ ◆

Zachary had so much wit about him. I laughed so hard at the many ways he came up with to tease and trick me. I loved to help him plot out fun tricks on Molly. She was always quick to play along to ensure the tricks were fully executed. Zachary was so pleased to make us laugh, and laugh we did. We spent the vast majority of our time laughing and playing with our son, and for that we are blessed. I remember some fun things with or about Zachary:

- Making coffee in the morning. We made lattés first thing each morning. How he watched for the first coffee drip to fall and would announce it to me by pointing, screaming, and nodding his head with approval. He liked to use multiple means of expression to communicate things he knew would please me (pointing, speaking, and nodding).
- Carrying him around the house every day for hours with him laying up on my chest or carrying him sitting in my hand, so he felt like he was moving about the house by his own power and direction.
- Zachary reeling in a fish and telling it 'bye as he let it go.
- Zachary driving my truck by standing in my lap and holding the steering wheel. Driving my truck, he would drag-race Molly in her van as she drove down the street next to us.

- How he would buck with anticipation when he was excited or in a hurry to get somewhere.
- Holding Zachary so he could watch out the window of our house for Molly's arrival back home from the store. He loved to see her come home and was so excited to see what she brought him. He would stand in the windowsill and watch the corner of our street. If it were dark, he would announce the mere presence of headlights from her car as they cast down the street.
- How he spoke in short sentences, words, and minimized syllables. This is because of his limited lung capacity.
- How he spoke to the world with his beautiful blue eyes. He could look right through you.
- How he loved to cook. He would assign a cheeseburger to each person as he cooked them on the grill.
- Him sitting on a table in a restaurant with our family and having so much fun. How he would order for himself something from the menu and then eat from your plate instead.
- Watching him play with his best friend Jodi Foose
- How he bossed around his brother and sisters
- He worried more about Heidi's well being more than any other thing. He loved her like no other, and I hope Heidi will always remember his love.
- How he wrestled with us all. He could roughhouse with the best of them.
- How he would to ride me like a bull. Zach was a great cowboy.
- The way he would laugh in a special way for Molly when she was teasing him.
- How he tried to imitate me yet had his own true identity.
- His expression when driving his power wheelchair. You could see in his eyes that he was thinking two rooms ahead of where he was and was planning something for when he got there.

- The way he loved to tease us all.
- Watching him trick Grandpa into changing Zach's diaper so he would then be naked and refuse to put another diaper on. He loved to be naked!
- The way he was never once ashamed of his physical appearance. He saw himself the same as we saw him, perfect!
- Watching him throw his diaper across the living room to show off. You just had to laugh at something like that.
- Watching him hold his blanket like he could not ever be separated from it and then leave it behind every time before going into a store or school because he wanted to show everyone how "big" he was.
- You only had to tell Zachary how to do something one time. He knew it forever after that. He was extremely smart.
- He was so talented at all the things he was capable of.
- Watching him play with Luke and Trey next door.
- Watching him climb the rocks on the fireplace with my help.
- How he shouted and pointed orders as we trained our hunting dog.
- He wore socks and never wore shoes.
- Opening and closing doors with him for hours.
- Watching him work the TV remote.
- How he made a point to impress Aunt Jackie and his cousins Jamie and Jessica.
- Working on the computer and playing computer games with him. He could work the computer system by using the mouse.
- The last few weeks of his life, I was amazed how he read single words.
- Singing the "Going on a Bear Hunt" song his mom taught him. And you had better get all the words right when you sang with him!

- How he impatiently waited on me when I was working on a home project for myself, but to the contrary, he was very patient if it was a project for him. He did not mind me being out in the garage for hours building his new bed frame. He was even more excited when he was able to help. He was so proud of the bed we built together.
- How proud he was of his room that mom, Kelly, and Carrie decorated for him. He would give all his visitors a tour of the room.
- Watching him draw and paint for us all.
- Having him explain over and over to me which school artwork hanging on the refrigerator was his and which was Heidi's.
- When he told me there was "wa-wa" down there as we looked out the window of an airplane flying over the Great Lakes.
- How he thought the best part of a vacation we took him on was the fact he had his family with him. He would name off all of us who went on the trip with him. People were so much more important to him than activities or places.
- The way he could not be separated from his service dog, Hobbs.
- Having him explain things to me.
- How he was more alert than everyone else, all the time. I so admired his intensity.
- Watching him do all the things his brother and sisters were doing. He would not be left out of anything.
- The way he insisted on drinking out of my glass.
- Watching in amazement at the number of donuts he could eat at his favorite donut shop.
- Zachary helping Molly with her work.
- Zachary typing on Molly's computer when he was not supposed to. It was like a movie where the hero is trying to get that secret data off a computer before some-

one walks into the room. He would work as fast as he could and constantly be checking the doorway for her to return.

- How he loved to go outside at sunset each evening.
- How he always loved what Molly bought him at the grocery store. He would pull the items from the grocery sack and thank his mom.
- The way he would jump from barstool to barstool in our kitchen.
- Helping him climb the stairs to get Heidi out of bed after naptime. He was so determined to climb those stairs and open her door.
- The way he knew where every obscure item in the house was when quizzed. I could ask him where the spatula was, and he could take me right to the drawer it was in.
- Having him listen in to your phone conversation from across the room and then say "goodbye" right before you did. That was his way of letting you know he was in tune with your conversation the whole time.
- The way we chased his grandparents down the street as they drove away after a visit.
- How he would run from the bed to the sofa and tease Courtney and Derek yelling "mine" as he dove to claim his favorite spot of the sofa.
- How he would proudly watch his brother or one of his sisters doing something new and/or fun and then yell out "me!" to let us know he wanted to try it also and join in on the fun or impress us with his abilities.
- Watching his brother Derek play in a basketball game and then insist that he come down out of the stands and play with the team on the floor. Zachary could only be a spectator for a short while and then he needed to participate.
- Playing hide and seek with his brother and sisters.
- Watching him sort all the colorful lures in his tackle box.

- Family camping trips at the lake.
- Watching Barney movies in the camper at the lake.
- When all of our family was in our bed and Zachary would jump on the bed and wrestle with us.
- Making a birthday cake for Heidi.
- The way he loved to go shopping with Molly and I.
- Having him tell me about his day at school with his mom and Hobbs and how he loved his teachers at school.
- The moment every evening when he shifted from "playtime with me" to "bedtime with mommy." During that time when Molly was preparing him for bed he did not allow me to touch him. Then once he was ready to lie down in bed he had to have me in the trundle bed next to his bed. If I was not ready for bed he waited up on me and would yell for me until I reported for bed-time.
- And the best moment of all, when Zach, Molly, and I said our prayers before going to sleep.

3½ *Years*

◆◆◆

3 ½ years is how long Zachary was with us. From the beginning 3½ was the number we were all trying to figure out. We were frequently asked how long is he expected to live? This is a number I guessed at each day. If I only knew the number I could then adequately plan for my actions with Zachary. The number danced around in my mind as I watched Zachary's health take a roller coaster ride, as I learned more about progeria, scientific research, and Zachary's form of progeria.

My mind chased the number around for many reasons. If only I knew he had a chance at a long life, I could be very conservative in his activities to ensure he would not get sick from exposure to others as a result of his weakened immune system. Or in contrast, if I knew he only had a short time to live I could throw caution to the wind and let him do anything and everything and enjoy the short time he would have. I guess looking back we kind of landed somewhere in between the two options. This was because we knew there was in fact a reasonable chance for treatment at a later time, but we also knew there was a likely chance Zachary could die at any time or certainly before any treatment or cure was discovered. Now I am faced with mixed emotions about our decisions, but if I had it to do over again, I would not change a thing.

When I realized that I would never know Zachary's lifespan until it was revealed in his final hour, I was able to accept I should treat every day as if it were the last. Shouldn't this apply to all of our lives? I suppose we are all trying to guess when our time on earth will be over.

Zachary's lifespan was difficult to predict because he had a more severe condition of progeria. We learned this by theory early on, since he developed symptoms earlier in age than the typical progeria patient, who usually exhibits symptoms at the age of two. Zachary exhibited symptoms at eight weeks of age.

Later we scientifically determined through the research of Dr. Jeffrey Miner at Washington University that Zachary's form of progeria was more severe. This was determined by performing RNA studies of Zach's cell lines in the laboratory. Still, with no other case to compare to, we could not put a number to the life expectancy. We could only assume it would be earlier than the thirteen years of age of the typical progeria case.

My guess of Zachary's life expectancy was five years of age. This number put Zachary's life on a tightrope in my mind. That was because five years was within the length of time I figured it would take to complete the research on potential treatment for progeria, meaning Zachary would live long enough to be included in the clinical study to treat or cure progeria.

About one month before Zachary's death, we scheduled his baseline study, which would prepare him for eligibility to participate in the treatment study. We were working with scientists to facilitate the clinical study process that was currently being researched on laboratory mouse models of the disease. The research was indicating success, and we were possibly within a few months of actually treating Zachary by this method. Thanks to research performed by Dr. Stephen Young of UCLA, it was demonstrated by laboratory testing that treatment with farnesyltransferase inhibitors significantly improved Zachary's damaged cells. Unfortunately, this was only performed as a research study on Zachary's cell line.

Zachary did not live long enough for the treatment to be tried on patients. However, Zachary and I talked about participating in the research, and I explained that although the research may not ever help him, it might one day help many other children. Zachary understood this reality and was very happy knowing he was helping others. Helping others made all our time and effort worthwhile even though Zachary was unable to be treated in time.

Although time ran out for Zachary, we remain grateful for the work the scientists and others helping with the research are accomplishing. I understood the research involved scientists working long hours in laboratories looking for answers and volunteers who gave up their previous careers and dedicated themselves to the race for a cure.

Molly and I were being very conservative in our care for Zachary to ensure that we did not jeopardize his condition before he was given this treatment opportunity. Our best efforts as parents did not overcome the fact it was Zachary's time to go. The key is it was our best effort and we did all we could to care for him, provide for him, and teach him about the Lord. That is the same we must do for all our children or even our family and friends.

Ephesians 6:4 Fathers, do not exasperate your children; instead, bring them up in the training and instruction of the Lord.

Having done all we can do for someone and should a loss still occur, we must then turn away from the past and look ahead to a time when we all will be together with our Lord in heaven. This is a way we can continue on with productive lives after the loss of a loved one. It won't be easy; even as I write this, I myself struggle with looking ahead and not dwelling on the way things were.

I remember how at times life was so urgent when I had Zachary. I mean things like his first trip to the zoo, buying him a toy he wanted, taking him fishing, and the many other things that a father desires to do with his son. It was urgent because I knew if I delayed, I might never get another chance.

Zachary and I were able to do everything we ever wanted to do in the time we had together. More time for more things together would have been great, but I have no regrets with the time we spent together. What a gift and comfort these feelings are to me now. I ask myself every day if I feel the same about my relationship with my other kids. Would I be satisfied if I had no more opportunities to accomplish things with them? Such is the struggle most parents are in as they prioritize their life.

My encouragement to others and even myself is to live with a sense of urgency to be happy with your kids. The rewards are great and even if you are not faced with the loss of your child as I with Zachary, you will never be able to get their childhood back once they are grown. You won't even be able to get the age of three back once they're four. Think about that and be motivated to love and spend time with your kids.

When Zachary was with me, I often pondered what it would be like should he pass away. I thought about what I would do, what life would be like, and how depressed I would be. Now that it is a reality and he has passed away, I find it is much like I figured it would be.

There were not many surprises, and I guess the thought of losing him at the time was so real I was able to already feel those feelings that would later come once I lost him. I cannot imagine going through such a loss without my faith in God.

It's interesting when you think about someone who is sentenced to death for the punishment of a crime they committed. To know you are going to die a scheduled death. a death at a certain time and by a certain means. It seems so extremely frightening to me to think about a situation of being given a death sentence. Then I think about how all our deaths are scheduled. We just don't know when or by what means. But we do know it is eventually coming. I wonder what is going through the mind of an inmate sitting on death row. Facing certain death, do they choose the righteous path? It seems difficult to understand how they could not choose the righteous path when they in fact know there death is coming.

Zachary's medical condition presented him a diagnosis of a scheduled death much earlier than a normal life span. Unfortunately, his death seemed to occur right on schedule with what nature had dealt him. I think about that event and how I had to watch him die just like we all eventually will. Death is a fact that we all will face. Death for each of us is just as certain as it was with Zachary, and just as certain as it is with a death row inmate. Knowing this, will we now choose the righteous path? The right answer seems so obvious but yet so difficult for us to act upon, even though it is all within our control.

With Zachary's medical condition, we knew there was a chance he would die at an early age. Of course my wife and I stayed positive in our thinking that he would overcome his illness and a cure would be in his future allowing him to live a long healthy life. It is difficult for a parent to know they may lose their child so young. We made an active choice and chose the righteous path for our situation. We did not live in anger with our situation; instead we thanked God for another day with our son. We lived each day glorifying God by loving and caring for our son. We kept a righteous attitude about Zachary. In return God gave us a son who in the face of life's challenges, reflected this righteous attitude for the world to admire.

I definitely am saddened when I think about how I had Zachary only 3½ years. But then I remember how many times I almost lost him sooner than 3½ years. It really was a miracle we had him for 3½ years. We prayed for the miracle to continue every day. We also prayed should it end, we would all understand and Zachary would go to heaven. It is amazing someone so young could have reached so many in such a short amount of time. Our minister, Richard Poe, reminded me Jesus' ministry here on earth was approximately 3½ years. This is evidence of the work that can be accomplished in a seemingly short amount of time.

Still it seems unfortunate when someone is doing such good work they should be called away from us. Could not the gospel have been grander if Jesus had his ministry on earth for 50 years instead of just 3½ years? It is not for man to say. The span of our lives is in the hands of God, and it is not known to man whether they are determined by a random system or whether they are intimately controlled by God.

Similarities lie with a family who loses their nineteen-year-old son in a war where he gives up his life with an act of courage.

Why couldn't he have accomplished this courageous act and then survived to do more good work? Nobody even had the chance to thank him before he died. Oh, don't be disheartened; the One who truly matters thanked him for the act.

A critical judgment we will each receive is what we did for our fellow man. For when we do kind acts for our fellow man, we are in essence doing them for God. I know that is what made Zachary so special to us all. Not because he had a rare disease and everyone felt sorry for him. But instead how he made us all feel in his presence or by merely reading or hearing about him. It is what Zachary did for his fellow man and how he was always concerned about how others felt rather than for his own pain or limitations. A quality so unexpected in a person who had so many immediate problems of his own. This quality of serving and caring about others is what we can learn from Zachary and many other special needs children. A good friend of mine once told me "life is about what you are able to do for others. Those are the things that really count." My friend is a very successful person. Yet, when I observed his life I could see considerable evidence he was indeed living his message. He enjoyed doing for others, and God had blessed him in return.

Likewise, Zachary's life is the example I am now trying to live up to. I also believe Zachary's conviction for loving his fellow man is what enabled him to overcome his daily pain and physical limitations. I know if Zachary could do it in the face of a terminal illness, we are all capable of doing the same no matter what our limitations are. And remember, we all will be rewarded ultimately.

We Must Keep Going

◆ ◆ ◆

When I consider my relationship with Zachary, I feel I was not so much a great parent as he was a great son. I was not able to save him from an early death, and that's something I will always regret. Zachary did not complain about his health. He might ask for a cool rag on his head to ease his many fevers or headaches. He might ask for a massage to ease the pain of his joint contractures. He might ask for lotion to make his skin feel better. However he did not whine or complain. I can tell you, I would not be so brave and enduring if I faced the same health conditions.

Now I am already panicking about our other children's health. It is the same day as Zachary's funeral and I feel like I am doing an inadequate job of caring for them. Will I ever feel like I am doing enough? I thought at the time I was doing enough for Zachary, but I was wrong. Zachary never let me down. He was always so much better than I was or am. This is such a humbling feeling for me as a parent to experience. The realization my child is a better person than I am. This is what truly made Zachary different in my perception. Not his physical appearance, health problems, or short duration of his life.

I recall the day I went to buy a newspaper because we knew they were printing a story about Zachary. I drove to a convenience store to purchase the newspaper from a coin-operated machine. As I parked my truck in front of the machine, I could see the view of the front page through the glass of the machine. I could see a huge photograph of Zachary and his sister Courtney. What an amazing feeling to see my kids on the front page, and they weren't even in trouble with the law! Needless to say, I was a proud parent as I read the story about Zachary and looked at his smiling photograph.

We always made sure we had plans ahead of us with Zachary: birthday parties, fishing trips, vacations, planting flowers in the garden, Super-Grover show, etc. We wanted to let Zachary know we wanted him to stay with us and nothing was more important than he was to us.

When Zachary died, we had many things planned for him within the next three months. We were scheduled to go to Orlando, Florida, to meet Barney; California to visit Hollywood Animals and his friend, Nelly the elephant; a fishing/camping trip to the lake with his grandparents; take his sister to see Super Grover, and undergo clinical trials for a treatment for progeria. In addition, an elephant was coming to visit him at his school so his schoolmates could also enjoy it, and we were planning Heidi's birthday party. Well, Zachary still got his way for Heidi's birthday party, and she had a cake with green "baby-bop" icing.

This planning was a normal couple of months of plans in Zachary's life. Therefore we do not wish we could have done any of these before he died. It is tough, though, to think we were perhaps within months of curing Zachary's condition. On that we can only hope the work Zachary, the scientists, and those who made contributions did will help other children with progeria. Molly and I continue to be active in the Progeria Research Foundation and other related research programs. We feel a strong connection to the current patients with progeria and are passionate about a cure for them and the future cases of progeria.

Molly called to let me know one of the kids from Zachary's class at school is very sick in the hospital. His mom has requested a visit from Zachary's dog Hobbs. Hearing this just made me fall apart emotionally, to the extent I would if it had been one of my own children who were sick. Molly is doing her part and will load up Hobbs and drive to the hospital to visit this child. Molly will no doubt remember the things she learned through Zachary and her faith and encourage this family with a visit. This is an emotionally difficult task since the child is in the same hospital in which Zachary was in a few weeks earlier.

Courtney and Derek came up with an idea for a bake sale fundraiser at their elementary school. They want to raise money for The Progeria Research Foundation. Today is the day of the bake sale. We spent yesterday evening baking cookies, brownies, and cupcakes for the sale. Even with the recent loss of their brother, they remain focused on helping other children. They are setting a great example and I am proud to see the motivation they have in this difficult time. They have never met another child who has progeria, but they are connected to all these children. They love them and care for them without ever having met them. They are proud of their brother and the work he did. Now they feel they must carry on the work Zachary was doing. They remind me of the Foose family who formed the California Chapter of The Progeria Research Foundation. They choose to live on continuing the work Amy Foose began. They will not be overcome by depression; instead, they will live productive lives by helping others. Jodi Foose came from Tulsa to help the kids sell items at the bake sale.

As I am overcome with sadness from missing Zachary, all I can do is turn it into positive actions. I must turn from this sadness and focus on caring and helping others. This will save me from being consumed by the sadness. Furthermore, this will let me rejoin Zachary when I go to be with my Lord.

Life certainly is not the same now that Zachary is gone. Zachary's last days in the hospital were a life-changing experience for me. It was like we were treading water in the middle of the ocean and were left in desperation to think such things as:

- should we swim for shore or wait in the water to be rescued;
- which direction should we even look for the shoreline to appear;

- do we focus on our final goodbyes, or do we focus on surviving;
- do we accept this is the end of our time on earth;
- what will things be like after what occurs next for us?

Now I am washed up on a beach today, and Zachary has been called on ahead of me. I have the choice of crawling up the beach and continuing on with my life, however nothing will be the same. Now events or problems in life occurring for me seem so meaningless. I listen to someone get stressed about work or other issues, and I think to myself how unimportant the issue really is.

Since losing Zachary I have not encountered a single issue that has made me feel nervous, anxious, stressed, or even excited. It is almost like I am numb and no occurrence can match what I have been through. It is difficult for me to extract any enjoyment out of life. It seems more enjoyable to reminisce about my times with Zachary. After experiencing an event such as losing Zachary so early in his life and making it through it, I feel that whatever is in the path ahead of me I will certainly overcome. Should I not overcome it, I refuse to let it hinder my work for the Lord in my remaining days.

A friend told me a story about how so many of the World War II veterans turned into extremely successful business leaders. This may be explained by after the challenges they had been faced with and surviving them, all other situations or stress in their life paled in comparison to anything the business world would later deal them.

Molly and I knew our fight to cure Zachary would likely be lost. We did not let that discourage us though. We fought hard to save him by providing the best care and seeking a treatment or a cure for him. We balanced this with letting him have the most fun he could have and help as many people as he could while he was with us. We can all reflect on Zachary's life and realize we are all terminal and are living lives with uncertain spans. We should all be able to turn the most desperate circumstances into rewards if not for ourselves, then others, as did Zachary.

I watched Zachary make it through extraordinary health issues, and all the while his attitude was that of which I will merely aspire to achieve. Zachary was my hero and my motivation while he was here. Zachary was truly a servant to the Lord. Remember, your attitude is a choice.

Zachary enjoyed opening and closing doors at our house. Over and over he would open and close a door while I held him or he sat by the door. It may be a bedroom door, a kitchen cabinet door, or even the microwave door. Molly told me maybe now he's in heaven helping Saint Peter with the gates.

Someone asked me, if I could have one wish, what it would be? When I consider the opportunity for such a wish, I come up with a set of rules that seem logical. Rules like the wish should be big, but realistic. Or perhaps the wish should deal with something you are actually involved in or directly impacted by. With this set of rules in consideration, I guess the standard wishes of "world peace" or "instant self wealth" are not applicable. Instead, I consider what has impacted me and to whom I owe a debt or gratitude. With that in mind, here is my wish:

> Children with progeria have given so much to me. They inspire me and show me how to truly live a righteous life, no matter the circumstances. They do so at such a high personal price. I wish I could in return simply make children with progeria healthy so they could experience life without the pain and difficulties they continually face.

Winning the Lottery

◆ ◆ ◆

Molly told me last night she has been asked what it is like to have a child diagnosed with a terminal disease. **She explains, "It is like winning the lottery."** Rather than being given a burden, she was given a blessing. God has given her a son who is to help save her soul and show her in the purest way the path God wants her on. She was tasked with caring and loving one of God's most special creations. It is the child who is burdened with the illness, and it is the parents' and world's duty and honor to provide love to all of God's creations. All will surely be rewarded for giving the love and care to children with special needs.

Matthew 18:10–14 See that you do not look down on one of these little ones. For I tell you that their angels in heaven always see the face of my Father in heaven. What do you think? If a man owns a hundred sheep, and one of them wanders away, will he not leave the ninety-nine on the hills and go to look for the one that wandered off? And if he finds it, I tell you the truth, he is happier about that one sheep than about the ninety-nine that did not wander off. In the same way your Father in heaven is not willing that any one of these little ones should be lost.

How We Did It

◆ ◆ ◆

Molly and I were faced with knowing our son had an extremely rare genetic disorder called progeria. There was no treatment or cure for this disease, and the average life expectancy was thirteen. However, Zachary had a more extreme form than the other twenty or so cases currently being studied. This meant Zachary's lifespan would likely be shorter. I estimated his lifespan at five years based on the research I had performed. There were no normal procedures for providing care for a child with progeria. Much of the care given was determined by our own decisions with help from medical professionals.

During his life, Zachary's maximum weight was 12 pounds and his maximum height was 32 inches. He was highly intelligent and mature, and we decided not to keep anything a secret from him. As he became aware of his condition and appearance, we explained the truth about his condition to him. We let him know he had a condition that made him sometimes feel sick and prevented him from walking. We explained details of the condition to him if and when they came up with him. Instead of focusing on what Zachary could not do, we focused on what he *could* do. This was the guidance and positive attention Zachary needed and deserved. Zachary was never afraid or bothered with the truth of his condition. The key to Zachary's courage was that Molly and I were proud of what and who Zachary was. We were not at all ashamed or embarrassed by Zachary's appearance. Quite the opposite in fact, we were proud of his abilities in spite of his physical limitations, which included his appearance. In our eyes he was our perfect son. This is how we raised Zachary, and as a result he was always proud of who he was.

We held such a high regard for our son that it was often difficult for us to see his physical problems. It seemed our eyes focused more on his positive attitude rather than physical aspects. We had to be vigilant in watching him for new health issues. He often would not tell us something new was wrong with him because he had become used to dealing with pain and health limitations. We had to be very observant with his health and discuss with him how he was feeling daily. We would often ask others who were not continually with him how he looked compared to the last time they saw him. Others were able to provide a more impartial opinion on how he appeared to be doing.

We chose to spoil Zachary with all our means. We gave him complete attention and worked hard for his everyday health care. Zachary simply wanted to have fun and be like his brother, sisters, and parents. He made it clear to us he wanted to go to school just like his older siblings, so that is what we did. We made him always feel equal and provided him everything he wanted. At the same time we were also raising Zachary to prepare him for a life that may be of a normal span. This was the right thing to do, and Zachary responded very well to his upbringing. I think as a result he felt normal but still very special and loved.

When at home, Zachary did not like to wear clothes because he was hot-natured. His head always felt hot to the touch. His thin skin and metabolism issues had much to do with this. He often preferred to be naked or to only wear a diaper. I am sure the first time someone met him it was a bit shocking to see this frail-bodied child exuberate so much life through his actions. Zachary was always proud of the way he looked, or maybe he just did not care what others thought about his appearance. We never insisted he wear clothes unless we were out in a public place in which clothes were expected of everybody. Zachary only liked to wear hats when he was in the bright sun. He was very light sensitive, and he used hats to keep the sun from his eyes. We wanted

Zachary to be as comfortable as possible. Zachary understood when clothes were required and was happy to wear clothes at these times. I always thought Zachary should dress in a way in which he was comfortable. I never considered covering a part of his body because someone may think he looked weird or be inclined to make fun of him. I figured if anyone had a problem with Zachary's appearance it was their own problem. I was proud of everything about Zachary, and everyone knew it. I loved the way Zachary looked because I truly loved him. However, I can understand if someone does not want to draw attention to their differences and chose to cover them with clothing items. By covering their differences with clothing, they can make it a non-issue and that is not a bad thing. I do think that is the individual's decision, though, and not so much the parents'. Molly and I chose to give Zachary every opportunity to live his life as openly as he chose to.

Zachary wanted to dress like us, and he did. He had favorite shirts and socks he preferred to wear. His favorite shirt was his "vacation shirt." This was an "aloha" shirt we had picked out together prior to one of our vacation trips. This shirt was special for many reasons. The first was likely because it was a bright flower print shirt that everyone noticed. The second was because he associated it with vacations and special events. Later, it seemed appropriate to choose to bury Zachary in his "vacation shirt." He also enjoyed wearing shirts that looked like shirts I wore. When asked about his shirt he would shake his head yes and say "just like Daddy."

One of Zachary's striking characteristics was his head. It was large compared to his body, and he had many visible veins. This is characteristic of a child with progeria. We never felt it necessary to cover his head up with a hat. I never felt right about concealing Zachary's appearance. Instead we did the opposite and let the world see him for what he really was. Besides, Zachary would not wear a hat on his head for very long unless it was needed for the sun or cold. Zachary was the Boss, so he always got what he wanted.

Molly and I never saw him as anything but beautiful. His brother and sisters did not realize just how different Zachary looked, because they could only see his inner beauty. They actually did not know he looked very different from other children until we talked to them about it.

Zachary never asked about lifespan or adulthood. He was content with the current events of his life. He was only concerned with the present and those he loved. Zachary loved to say his prayers with his family. He told me everyday how he loved God. Zachary never questioned his health or physical limitations. I wondered if he would as he watched his little sister pass him in physical development. She became double his weight by six months of age. When she started crawling, it certainly changed Zachary, and he wanted to imitate her. He was able to crawl with my help. The same was true when she started walking. Hours were spent each day with me supporting Zachary's weight with my hand, allowing him to walk around with Heidi. I would follow behind Zachary on my knees with my hand under his bottom and he did the rest. I did everything I could to make each moment for him as satisfying as I could. With my help he did all the things a three-year old wanted. He would walk, run, and climb. He had so much desire to do those things, and then when he watched his little sister begin to do those things he would not be denied. He would try so hard, and I remember him standing with me holding his hands so he could support his own weight as long as he could. His legs would begin to tremble and he would let me know to help him again. He would smile so proudly for himself as he walked a few feet across the floor, and our family would clap for him. Considering how physically challenged Zachary was, I was often amazed at his abilities. Surely if his talents were present in a body of perfect health he would be a great athlete. I think such talent is often the case for many physically disabled people, and it serves to teach us about the power of utilizing our God-given abilities. I have witnessed numerous physically disabled individuals who were able to accomplish amazing things.

Zachary knew he looked like the other kids with progeria. He saw some kids with progeria on a television show and watched with great interest. When I asked what he thought about those kids Zachary simply answered "me!" When he finally met another child with progeria he was instantly her friend and so very content to play with her.

Zachary treated his older brother and sisters often like a parent and other times like a true little brother. He treated Heidi, his baby sister, as if she was his own baby. He looked out for her and required to know where she was at all times. As she grew larger in size than he was, he began to treat her more like a sister, a twin sister I suppose. Although he never lost that guardian responsibility over her, Zachary was a better parent to Heidi than I was.

The first thing Heidi and Zachary asked for was each other when they awoke each morning. Courtney, Zachary's older sister loved him so much that most of her playtime was spent entertaining him. She always made sure Zachary was included in whatever activity she was doing. Here is a poem that Courtney wrote after Zach's death.

"I Am"
I am a tall girl wondering about life.
I wonder if a kid could do everything.
I hear the railroad track roar at night.
I see the cows running in a herd across the field.
I want a shopping mall only for our hearts.
I am a tall girl wondering about life.

I pretend to be a bug learning to be safe.
I feel that a wondering snake is slithering up my legs.
I touch the cloud that blocks the sun.
I cry when I think of my brother.
I am a tall girl wondering about life.
I understand that life doesn't always stand.
I say that my brother's spirit haunts me.
I dream that I will see him again someday.
I try to make my heart bigger.
I hope that someday my dreams will come true.
I am a tall girl wondering about life.

Derek, Zachary's big brother, loved to tease Zachary in a playful way and was always there to protect him and look out for him. Derek did not like to be separated from Zachary. He was always eager to give Zachary "little treasures" he had. From his favorite toys cars to rocks and leaves, Zachary was always happy to accept these gifts and was equally as proud to have them.

Lindsay, Zachary's oldest sister was so proud of him. She thought he was the coolest kid. She would paste pictures of Zachary on her folders at school and would brag to her friends how smart he was. He felt so important when she would call to talk to him. Zachary was always so impressed with Lindsay and loved to think of her as a stand-in mother since she was the oldest. Our children learned that we all have something in common with people with disabilities. We all have a heart and feelings. Most parents don't teach their children about how to treat people that are different from them. You can hear them say "stop starring" instead of telling them to smile and say hello. Children take "stop starring" as don't look and then try not to make eye contact with the person, making the person with the disability feel even more different and self-conscious. Our children have learned to smile and say hello, because although everyone was created different, no matter their appearance, we are all children of God.

Zachary had an amazing passion for school. Early on I thought he might never attend school. But he understood what school was, and he let Molly know he wanted to start attending. He was an exceptional student. He was so proud of his school-work and the songs and stories he learned there. He also enjoyed church and attending Sunday school with the other kids.

Zachary was the boss of our house, and he controlled our lives for the most part. Amazingly, his control always led us to happiness as a family. We let him decide many things by asking him what he wanted to do. We gave him much freedom to guide us and shape our activities so he would be happy. In letting him do so, he never disappointed us.

I never actually heard any person say something insulting about Zachary. I was always prepared for my reaction should this occur, but I am thankful to my fellow man that nobody ever said harsh words about my son in my presence. This is remarkable, considering that I took him almost everywhere I went. I never hesitated taking Zachary somewhere because I thought he might not be accepted or there might be individuals there who would not understand his situation. I was always pleasantly surprised at everyone's acceptance of him. I decided long ago that anyone's criticism of Zachary would never be acceptable behavior to me. I think this attitude of mine was apparent and people respected that. Instead of keeping him away from such potential situations, we did the opposite. We went out into the world every day and discovered that society welcomed Zachary with love and understanding. So many people became his friends and went out of their way to help him.

We traveled on trips together several times, went shopping and out to dinner frequently, and attended all kinds of events. And I mean *all* kinds of events. Zachary went to weddings, parties, plays, shows, rodeos, gun shows, boat shows, circuses, aquariums, museums, zoos, wildlife parks, and anything else that would entertain him.

When I was out with Zachary I carried him in my arms boldly, proudly, and lovingly. Perhaps to some this was intimidating, but I hope that most found it heartwarming. Thinking back now, I wonder how we were perceived as we did things together, and it would be interesting to know the thoughts that secretly went through people's minds. Most of the input we received was from people letting us know what a great example we were setting and this meant a lot to us. We were happy to share Zachary with the rest of the world and risk facing opposition to his appearance at the chance of helping others and his own confidence and happiness. It turned out that the world was always there for us and received Zachary with loving and open arms.

He was definitely in the public eye much more than the average kid. In fact, Zachary had celebrity status. Practically everyone in our state knew of him, and most of the people in our town knew him personally. I have always been impressed with the overall treatment and respect he received. It exceeded any previously conceived expectations I had. People were great to him.

From time to time, we did encounter people who asked some peculiar or inappropriate questions, but I always ascribed this to their inability to say the right thing. And that is an excusable act, because I could tell they meant well.

One of the best things Molly gave me was the knowledge that Zachary was safe and in great care when he was not with me. Molly was always there for Zachary, and it meant everything to me. I am forever thankful to Molly for being the strong one during the times I could not.

Zachary was always so satisfied with the life he lived. He was satisfied no matter the circumstance. This seemed truer each day of his life. He was able to extract so much joy out of simple things. Especially time spent with his family and friends. He truly had life figured out. He was content and happy in spite of his challenged life. Even with all his physical problems he continued to focus on making others happy. Although our life was completely about providing for Zachary, he was all about caring for others. *He was like a perfect pool of water that would reflect everything back, perhaps even more elegantly than the real image itself.*

We received a letter of condolence from a person who commented on how they wish they had made it to Zachary's third birthday party. They received an invitation and planned on attending. Instead, they let something get in the way, and they did not make it to the party despite their original plans. We certainly understood this person not making it to the party. There were many people who said they would be there but did not show up. We know people have busy lives and can't attend every event they would like to. However, I did find it interesting how this person expressed such a desire to be at the party and even more regret they did not attend.

In contrast, Zachary acquired a friend a year earlier named Holly. She lived in Arkansas about 200 miles away. She became interested in Zachary after seeing him on television. She began writing letters to him and they became great friends through the letters. As I read the letters to Zachary, this young girl's feelings of compassion and love were evident. She really cared for Zachary and made an effort to let him know it. I was amazed when she traveled such a distance and arrived at his birthday party. She was very pleased as Zachary sat on her lap. Her efforts did not end after the birthday party. Again how happy it made me as I noticed her and her parents at Zachary's funeral. We later sent her one of Zachary's favorite stuffed toy animals to remember him by.

I think about my own life and how I often let unimportant things get in the way of my plans. I let myself be occupied with activities that prevent me from doing what I need to be doing. The lesson learned is we should prioritize our lives so we are spending time doing what really matters to us. We can do this by searching our heart and asking ourselves what we really want and then following through. I am so easily distracted off my planned path that I find it helpful to write down what it is I really want to do and accomplish. This helps me stay on my planned path. I often wonder what good things I have missed out on because I was off doing something that really was not a worthy activity.

Living Righteously

$$\blacklozenge\,\blacklozenge\,\blacklozenge$$

I now must live my life serving the Lord and looking forward to the day when Jesus comes back. I must do all I can, so when the day arrives I will not crouch down and feel like hiding or perhaps scrambling to complete unfinished business. Instead, I will look up to heaven and rejoice in the moment, because I will be ready. I will be ready to see the Lord and be judged for my work. That is my plan, and I must remind myself daily and pray I remain on this course.

My purpose here on earth is to do work satisfying to God. This may include a broad range of activities. The key is to try to always be doing righteous work and performing righteous actions. Should I fail, I will ask for forgiveness and try again. I must make sure that whatever I spend my time doing, it must be righteous. This may consist of spending time with my family, providing for my family through work, or the obvious good tasks of helping others and learning more about God's will.

The key is having God's interest in mind in all things I do and not my own self-serving interests. It goes back the fact that my purpose here on earth is to get to Heaven with Jesus.

When I became a parent, I also assumed responsibility to assist my kids with the knowledge and confidence to do God's work in their lives.

Psalm 78:5–7 He decreed statutes for Jacob and established the law in Israel, which he commanded our forefathers to teach their children, so the next generation would know them, even the children yet to be born, and they in turn would tell their children. Then they would put their trust in God and would not forget his deeds but would keep his commands.

Give yourself a test: If something were to happen to your children, will you have regrets? Will you be happy looking back on what you did with them or for them? Will your final moments with them hold you over until you're together again in heaven? Constantly ask yourself these questions. Within hours of Zachary's death, I was asking myself these questions in regards to my other children. I am now struggling again with the answers to those questions.

Likewise, I should be trying to provide the same for all those around me. The state of living I strive for is one in which my efforts and time are not completely consumed with working on myself but getting a handle on my own self and therefore having more time to dedicate to others, especially my children. For how can you help others if you cannot help yourself or even if you fall so short as spending all your time on yourself? I have lived for so long spending all my time on myself. I watched as opportunities passed me by for years. I was consumed with myself. Then on July 7, 2002, I was blessed with Zachary. He taught me and provided me a platform that I might focus on someone other than myself. Every day my walk with God was furthered along as I spent time with Zachary. Zachary was a wonderful living example of righteousness. That is why I felt inferior to my son and I would not prefer it any other way. What a true blessing Zachary was in my life! He was my hero here on earth who enlightened my path to God. He did this every day of his life and never fell short. I will never be able to match his example as I strive to help my family and friends; I will only aspire to be as great as Zachary.

Zachary did not cry in his last days, and he especially did not cry as he fought during his last moments, even though his last days and certainly his final moments were extremely challenging. Molly and I witnessed all he went through and held him, encouraged him, and helped him as he went through the medical challenges of his last days. It is hard to understand how a 3½ year old boy could be so courageous. Zachary left this world brave and confident, just the same as he lived each of his days.

I think back about how Zachary had so many things he liked to do and say. He had so much personality and charisma. I see this same quality in Megan and Sam. These children also have progeria. I hear the stories from the families of those who have passed away as a result of progeria, Amy Foose and Ronnie. I watch home videos of them, and it is so apparent they too had this charisma. Through just one photograph, I could see the same personality in Nigel. The photograph was a black and white snapshot of him in a tree he had climbed in a local orchard. He proudly smiled, sitting on the limb of the tree.

Special needs children are often brilliant and intriguing people. They can teach us and demonstrate to us life at its best. If you don't believe me, consider how you felt after an illness or brush with death. After having the flu for a week do you somehow appreciate things around you a bit more? After avoiding a car wreck that would have resulted in certain death, does your perspective on life seem suddenly clear to you? Do you go home and cherish your relationship with your family like never before, now that you were reminded not to take it for granted? I encourage everyone to develop a relationship with a special needs person through volunteering with a support organization or maybe just starting a friendship with such a person. They may be able to show you the perspective on life you are missing.

I lived my life for thirty years in a primarily self-serving manner. My work and efforts seemed to center around doing for myself and then for others, if I could fit them into my schedule. I was a nice guy for the most part, but I was in a pattern of making selfish choices. When I consider the lives of special needs children, it seems to me they are living so unselfishly as an example for us all to behold. They each have qualities so honest and pure. I feel guilty that it took a terminally ill and handicapped child to open my eyes to making unselfish choices. I always understood the righteous path in life before but refused to always accept the path. It was far too easy for me to instead compromise when faced with life's choices and challenges. Zachary taught me to never allow myself to compromise when faced with making the right decision. Such compromises will eventually lead you astray. By compromising when challenged, we are not living up to our potential. The rewards are endless when we live up to our potential and the choice to do so is our own.

When we consider all the good work and positive impact Zachary had on so many people, we try to understand and make some sense of his life. Although Zachary was so weak in health, he was so very strong spiritually. As a parent I cannot take the credit for his spiritual strength. At times, Zachary was the teacher, and I was inspired by him. My wife asked if it was possible Zachary were an angel sent to help us. He did certainly help us, and he certainly was angel-like. I consider this, and of course I do not know the answer nor does it really matter. Perhaps he was not an angel but just had living a righteous life figured out from the start. Maybe he was merely doing the right thing and simply not compromising when challenged in life. The same capabilities we all have and when these capabilities are practiced it appears as if an angel has landed on earth.

I loved Zachary's power wheelchair. More specifically, I loved how the wheelchair moved through our house under the power controlled by Zachary. I loved seeing the pleasure on his face as he controlled where he was going. For a child who was out of control of his physical health and destiny, Zachary sure was in control of his life and that is what made him so righteous. This is also why so many loved him and looked up to him.

Your Faith is Visible

$\blacklozenge\,\blacklozenge\,\blacklozenge$

How can it be that a child so young and small can show such a great faith? Trying to make sense out of Zachary's life leaves me with many questions. Could he have been such a model of faith and love had he been born healthy or, more broadly, "free of problems?" How tragic it is that many of the apostles died a martyr's death through persecution of their faith. But what an example of faith it has shown us. When challenged, they peacefully laid down their lives providing an example that this life is not as near important as our eternities. God did not promise a life free of challenges or even tragedy.

I believe God created a world where challenges will occur or at least be allowed to occur. Every one of us will definitely be challenged. Some will be challenged more than others, and that is why it is said life is not fair. The scale of your challenges may not be fair, but your choices to deal with the challenges are fair. For some it will not take much of a challenge to break their spirit, while others will persevere against unimaginable challenges. Our challenges will be dictated by factors such as health, environment, family, time, or even random occurrences. The point is when you are challenged what will you do to address and overcome it? What you should do is often simple and easy, but accepting this is not always so easy. God allows the devil to tempt us in many ways. But the truth is that there is only one right way, and it is God's way. Search your heart, pray, study your Bible, and open your mind for God's answer to your challenges. Your reward for doing so is eternal, and that is the key to overcoming life's challenges.

Parents and caregivers of special needs children are the lucky ones. They are the ones who have an opportunity to be with an angel right here on earth. Just by doing all you can for these children and dedicating your focus to them, you can be assured you are doing God's work. But that's not all. Here is the best part: just by caring for these children you can and will impact many others, particularly if you are able to provide this care in the public eye. You may never realize the positive impact you will have on others by setting this example. We are all surrounded by popular notions that try to program us to be selfish. By just by being at a grocery store, community event, restaurant, church, or other public place with your special needs child, you are probably going to touch someone else's heart.

We saw this occur many times when we were with Zachary. There were times when we would be enjoying a nice dinner at a restaurant with Zachary and the family, and Zachary refused to sit in a high chair since he was not a baby, although he was the same. If he sat in a chair, the table would be at eye level with him, so he chose to sit right on top of the table! He would be sitting in his favorite spot, which was the center of the table top, scooting around to everyone's plate and sampling any food he found inviting. This position at the table also allowed him to be involved in all conversations that occurred. He was involved in everything. He even insisted on getting my credit card out from my wallet and handling payment for the meal. Our dinners out were always such a great time for the family!

While we were having a dinner at a restaurant, a person or family often would approach the table and introduce themselves and start up a conversation about Zachary and comment on how wonderful it was to witness our family and they might even share how inspired they were by seeing us. This was amazing to me, because we were just out having dinner. We were not trying to change someone's life, but we often did. We did this by setting an example by showing our love for our family.

The same thing would happen while shopping at one of the many other places we frequented. You might not realize it at the time, but when you are with a special needs child, many people are watching you to see how you are dealing with your situation. There are people all around you that are seeking inspiration, and you have the opportunity and gift from God to show them what they need to witness. That is what makes these children "special" to the world.

After Zachary passed away, we were at our local grocery store, and one of the workers was telling us how much they missed seeing Zachary shopping at the store. We would let Zachary use his power wheelchair to explore the store and pick out the items he wanted. He had so much fun racing around in his wheelchair at the grocery store. I never really noticed the workers at the store watching Zachary. Come to find out, the worker let us know they would all gather in the break room of the store and watch the security video tape so they could see Zachary operating his wheelchair and having so much fun the way he always did. They were all so intrigued by him, and this provided them with inspiration. We never knew we were being watched at the time, but what a lesson in knowing that others are watching you and how you manage your life with your child. This was a secret surveillance approach these folks had. It just goes to prove you can be sure others will be watching you and how you deal with life's challenges.

The lesson we gained from having a child with special needs is that you have been given an opportunity, the stage is set, many eyes are on you, and now you can help others simply by helping and loving your child. The numbers you will help may be many and you may never know it when it occurs. All of this comes through the simple act of loving your child with all your capability. What a gift you are given. That explains why when Molly is asked what it is like having a special needs child she can answer, "It's like winning the lottery!"

We realized what a blessing we were given the entire time we had Zachary. We embraced who he was and did as much good work for him and through him as we could while he was alive with us. These blessings and abilities have been the most difficult parts of losing Zachary. The opportunity for these occurrences to inspire others through our son is gone with Zachary. Now we find ourselves trying to set the same example with our other healthy children. The effects are the same, but they are not nearly as far-reaching. We have found a strong urge to be involved with other special needs children, just days after Zachary's death. The rewards of the work with special -needs children are so great for us we felt compelled to do so.

I look at a photograph taken four months ago, when we were at The Progeria Research Foundation workshop held in Boston. The photo was taken of Zachary and his friend Megan, who also has progeria. They met for the first time while in Boston, and they were instant friends. They look so much alike, and they both realized it immediately. As I look at the photo I am proud to say I feel the same way about Megan as I did Zachary. I love her so much and I hope the next time I see her again that she has been cured. She and her family deserve it so much and I am so thankful for the parents she has. They have done a lot of great work for the Progeria Research Foundation. They are the ambassador family for the foundation. It did not take Megan long to start liking me. She watched me for about ten minutes and observed the way Zachary and I were together, and she decided I was going to be her new friend. I was so happy she felt this way, because I wanted her to like me so much. She immediately treated me like she had known me for a long time, and I'm sure that is credited to when she observed the way I treated Zachary. I remember how content I felt when I held Zachary with one arm and Megan with the other arm and ran through the hotel lobby with the two of them shouting joyfully as they bounced in my arms. This moment was certainly a highlight of my life.

It amazes me how Zachary hit it off with Megan's brother and sister. Zachary could sense their understanding of him and the way they instantly loved him. Zachary really wanted to impress Megan's older brother. He really put on a show of how mischievous he could be the first evening he met them at a dinner party in Boston. There was a can of straws on the table, and he threw one on the floor. Megan's brother laughed at him approvingly.

Zachary picked up on that and immediately began throwing straws off the table as fast as he could. Everyone at the table began to laugh and cheer him on, and he went on to entertain them all with a straw-throwing display only outdone by the smile on his face while he performed. Zachary did the same with the Foose family and the other families of children with progeria. I remember Zachary playing with Jodi and Chip Foose, siblings of Amy Foose who also had progeria. Zachary would lay on the floor with Jodi and a large pile of candy. He would unwrap each piece of candy and insist Jodi taste it as he placed the candy in her mouth. He laughed at the many reactions Jodi gave for each piece of candy. And then there was the breakfast at an upscale restaurant where Zachary and Chip threw sugar packets back and forth until a full-scale sugar packet fight erupted. Nobody said anything about the disturbance, because the Boss could get away with anything.

I would give anything to be able to see the progress of a treatment for Megan and the other kids with progeria. I think a lot about the week we spent in Boston working with the scientific team on finding a cure or treatment for progeria, and the time Zachary was able to spend with Megan, age five, and Sam, age nine. Sam was so lovingly concerned for Zachary the day he met him. He was always asking how Zachary was feeling. He obviously inherited the quality of caring for others from his parents, who led the Progeria Research Foundation.

In my mind, I can still see the three of them sitting in the hotel lobby, drawing cars with car design expert Chip Foose, playing, chasing, eating candy, and making a lot of noise. I watched in amazement as people would approach our group and want to meet the kids. They were in awe of how happy they were. I watched as the word of these kids actually flowed from the hotel lobby and into the streets. People started coming in for their chance to meet these intriguing children. Before long a crowd had formed around the kids and people asked to meet the kids and have their photograph taken with them. As the people left, they told us how inspired they were by watching these kids enjoy themselves and hear their stories. Those few hours were perhaps the most sacred time of my life. I witnessed a spectacular event spent with awesome people. All humbled by the presence of these three children. These children in my eyes were perfect.

I know heaven holds a special place for these special children. Zachary had faith and was an innocent and honest child. How did he have faith in the face of a life filled with tremendous pain and health difficulties? He was surrounded by a world of people filled with and sharing their faith and love. This is the good side of living with progeria. It brought out the goodness in all the people around him. Our home was filled with faith in God and true love, not just within our family, but also from all those who entered our home either by chance or to visit with Zachary. With just one look into Zachary's eyes, all those who approached cast upon him their love and affection. Our friends in the scientific research and medical communities worked so hard for him, and he knew it. Those who saw him on television responded with cards and letters, and Zachary read of their love. Those in the church who heard of him continually prayed for him, and Zachary heard of this and was happy. Our son was literally surrounded by a world of love for him. How could he not be filled with good faith when blessed with such treatment from everyone in his life? This love and kindness from others made him so strong and happy. It is proof to the true effectiveness to the scripture:

1 Corinthians 13:13 And now three remain: faith, hope, and love. But the greatest of these is love.

This type of action really works and is especially effective when done in entirety. It is often said that children with Progeria are extra special people and there is just something mystical about them. I am convinced that these children are so special because of the way their fellow man loves them. They are loved the way God wants us to love everyone. In fact they are completely enveloped in this love. This is because it is obviously recognized by all those who interact with them that they deserve to be loved perfectly. The compassion can't help but be brought out when you see a very small child and it is very apparent their health is suffering. The result of all this good treatment from others is a life that is reflective of what God wants for us all. The shame is that it takes a child with a terminal illness for the world to get the commandment "love thy neighbor as thy self" right. I am convinced that if everyone would treat others the way they should we could all experience this happiness. And I have to admit I have figured this out from watching Zachary's life and comparing to it to those very near him and then looking outward. I look at the people right next to Zachary, his siblings. I consider how they are treated compared to Zachary and I see and imperfect reaction. As a parent I went to great effort to treat Zachary perfect. I don't always treat his siblings the way I should. I struggle with parenthood the same as most parents. From this very basic level in my own life I know that any flaws I have in the treatment of those near to me will have an effect as my children's lives are shaped. One can surely expand this logic all the way up to how we treat one another. It ultimately impacts us all even spreading to how various countries and cultures treat each other. Zachary taught me what is attainable if we all follow God's will and treat each other with love and compassion.

Celebrate Life

◆◆◆

Zachary's memorial service was held at the church in our hometown. The church truly loved Zachary and did so much for him throughout his life. At the memorial services our minister, Richard Poe, presented the service. Richard spoke of Zachary's accomplishments and read entries of his life from our journal. Others at our invitation also spoke about Zachary. It was truly a day to celebrate his life.

Jodi Foose spoke of her friendship with Zachary and how he helped her achieve closure with the loss of her sister, Amy, who had died from progeria twenty years earlier. Jodi often visited Zachary, and when he became sick she was there for him.

Zachary's teacher spoke of how he enjoyed school. She told of how Zachary and his dog Hobbs shaped the dynamics of the school. She let everyone know Zachary loved to sing school songs, read stories, and most of all paint. She thanked Molly and me for letting Zachary attend school and live his life. She confirmed these decisions were what Zachary wanted and the result was the betterment of many lives.

Audrey Gordon of The Progeria Research Foundation spoke of when she met Zachary in Boston and how he captured the hearts of the research scientists. She spoke of the foundation's desire to continue to strive for the health of other children with progeria and of how thankful she was to be included in the service to honor Zachary and to know our family would continue to support their efforts to find a cure even though it was too late for Zachary.

Zachary's cousin Jamie read a poem at the service, and all of his family was there just as they always were for him.

The Oklahoma County Sheriff's Honor Guard stood beside Zachary's casket at the funeral. At the graveside service they did a twenty-one-gun salute and presented Molly with his sheriff's deputy badge and the American flag they placed over Zachary's casket during the funeral. Zachary was shown much honor by these activities. It was evident Zachary was the Boss to many and he was certainly respected to the highest level.

The Oklahoma County Sheriff's and Stillwater Police Department provided the escort for the funeral. They did a tremendous job with the funeral, truly honoring Zachary. Our church family and especially our neighbor Kelly did a great job coordinating the funeral, as did his friend Daniel with the singing.

There were several hundred in attendance at Zachary's funeral service. For Zachary's funeral, people traveled to Oklahoma from three coasts, mountains, and many states in between these places. Seeing Zachary's numerous friends at the funeral made me think back at how I hoped others would come to know what a blessing Zachary is to this world. The attendance of Zachary's funeral; the cards, letters, and flowers we received; and the charitable gifts to the organizations he represented made it evident my hopes were exceeded.

I cried enough while Zachary was alive that I did not need to cry at his funeral. Instead I enjoyed honoring his life and celebrating his new life with the Lord. Zachary was loved and many understood the blessings he gave to us. I was proud of my son as I followed his casket being carried out of our church and everyone remembered his life. I had walked past the pews in our church many times before for worship service carrying Zachary in my arms and feeling the same way. Before we left the church, some of Zachary's teachers released purple balloons in honor of him.

Tribute

— ◆ ◆ ◆ —

It was really neat to see our town decorated in purple ribbons and balloons in honor of Zachary. Purple was his favorite color. Every mailbox in our neighborhood had a purple ribbon. Every Federal Express truck had a purple ribbon. Many local businesses had tied purple ribbons on their doors. There were even purple ribbons tied to cars in town. Outside of Zachary's doctor's office the nurses had tied purple balloons to the trees. There were also purple balloons outside Zachary's favorite donut shop, and they also sent flowers in his honor. They loved him and told us they still love him. I remember how the girls at the donut shop would bring fresh donuts out especially for Zachary. I still do not understand how a boy who weighed twelve pounds could eat almost two donuts for breakfast. The ratio of donut to boy is astounding! Do the math for yourself. The donut shop made a batch of donuts with purple icing in honor of Zachary. I'd never seen a donut with purple icing and I know Zachary is pleased with their gesture.

I dropped Courtney and Derek off at school this morning. Their first day back since Zachary's passing away. Every kid walking into the school was wearing purple. Purple was Zachary's favorite color. I looked through the glass front to the school lobby. I could see more purple clothes on children and purple balloons floating. They all wore purple to please Zachary. This was Courtney and Derek's school, not Zachary's. Zachary often visited the school for his siblings' school events. Molly, Zachary, and Hobbs also spoke at the school about special needs children so all the children at the school knew Zachary well. I am proud to see all the kids pleasing Zachary now after he did his best during his life to please all of us. Zachary received hundreds of cards from these kids and it was obvious they cared for him. What a great show of affection for him and his brother and sister. Zachary made a difference and brought many closer to God.

The following are some of the tributes to Zachary presented at his funeral service.

Tribute by Malinda O. Webb, M.D., Zachary's personal physician:

As a pediatrician, I really have a wonderful job. Most days I get to witness the miracle of new life. I get to watch kids grown and help them feel better. Sometimes my job is heartbreaking because not every child gets to grow up without pain or diseases. I also have a job that involves lifelong learning. I learn from each and every patient and each and every loss. I don't often get the opportunity to pay tribute to my patients and their families to let them know how much they have taught me and helped me grow. I am grateful to Zachary's family for allowing me this tribute.

Zachary and his family have certainly contributed to my growth as a physician (not to mention the growth of my gray hairs). Not only have I learned a great deal about a very rare and debilitating condition, but I have also learned about living. Zach did not have typical progeria. His defect is so very rare and serious that he probably shouldn't have survived beyond the first few weeks of gestation (pregnancy). He came into the world fighting the odds and, apparently, went out the same way. Zach was one in a billion. He was a true miracle. We joked about calling his disease the "Zach Attack" and I still think that fits. Zachary didn't really like coming to our medical office. I don't think he liked me or my staff even when Hobbs was there to make it better. That didn't stop us from falling in love with him or worrying to death about him. We all knew we were witnessing a miracle as well as history, and we were honored to be a part of his life.

Molly and Keith and the rest of the family are also a great inspiration. They have taken a devastating illness and turned it into an opportunity to educate others as well as help Zach. They taught me what it means to be a true advocate. They worked hard to make sure Zach lived as full a life as possible. They taught about hope in the face of devastation. They never doubted that a cure was possible and made sure they knew everyone that could was involved with progeria research. Molly even taught me a thing or two about handling those difficult insurance companies.

Zachary will be sorely missed, but never forgotten. The scientist part of me will always be grateful that he taught me about progeria and Lamin A genes and inhibitors; the physician part of me will continue to agonize that I could have done more. The human part of me will be humbled by the miracle of Zach and love him always.

Tribute by Kirsten McIntyre, News Anchor for KWTV News 9:

I will never forget the first time I saw Zach. It was actually a picture. I was standing in my newsroom at Channel 9 and had just been assigned to Zach's story. One of my producers had received a forwarded e-mail, along with a picture, about a little boy in Still-water who needed a service dog. Knowing I have a soft spot for children, my producer told me I should prepare myself before I made the 60–mile trip. He opened the attachment and I could not believe my eyes. At 2-years-old, Zach weighed less than 10 pounds. His little arms and legs could no longer straighten because of arthritis. He only had a few strands of hair. Zach was an old man in a little boy's body. Yet, he was smiling. I cried that day. It would not be the last time.

I was in high school when I decided to pursue a career in broadcasting. My decision was probably based on two really bad reasons. One, I did not know what else to do, and two, I liked public speaking. Never mind I was a terrible writer and had a southern drawl I had perfected while growing up in small-town Oklahoma. Now, after being in broadcast news for fourteen years, I know why God placed me in this career. I love stories of inspiration. I never get tired of seeing how one person's story can touch people in such a way they are compelled to make a difference. My little buddy Zach was one of those stories.

It seemed like overnight Zach gained rock star status. Every-where he went, people wanted to know if he was the little boy on television or in the newspaper. Complete strangers became com-mitted to making sure he got his service dog. Schoolchildren sent their allowance money. One woman wrote a check for ten thou-sand dollars. Letters and cards flooded in from everywhere, includ-ing a prison. Zach had even moved on the hearts of men who were supposedly hardened by crime. All pretty amazing for a little boy who was so small, he could sit in the palm of his daddy's hand.

I think my favorite memory of Zach was on his third birth-day. I may have been more excited than the birthday boy. A few days before, Molly had mentioned to me Zach had been asking for a helicopter ride. (He had no memory of an earlier emergency flight from Stillwater to Tulsa because he was so sick.) When Molly said that, I thought to myself, "Umm . . . we have a helicopter." The wheels started turning and when I asked my news director, Blaise Labbe, he gave me the "let's make it happen" look. Our pilot, Mason Dunn, came in on his day off, and we flew to Stillwater to make a birthday wish come true. Oklahoma State University even let us land on their soccer field. It was a day I will never forget! It was pure joy!! Zach was so excited he hardly uttered a word the entire time we were in the air. Zach was a News 9 favorite. We all knew his birthdays were numbered and we wanted number three to be extra special. We were blessed to share in what would be his last one.

I saw Zach just a few days before he went to be with Jesus. I took him a News 9 helicopter model and promised him another ride when he got out of the hospital. It was something to have him look forward to and to keep fighting. At that point, I would have promised him the world. I never gave up hope but I knew his little body was getting tired. I'll never forget the night he died. Our mutual friend, Jodi Foose, called and said, "We lost him." What do you say? All I could utter over and over were the words, "I am so sorry."

I am still sorry about the death of my special friend, but I am not sorry I had the honor and privilege of knowing him during his short life. He blessed me in so many ways. Even when he did not feel good, he would make me smile with his cute little giggle. He gave me a flower which I keep on my desk at work. It is my reminder to take the time to smell the roses. We are not guaranteed tomorrow. Every day has to count. He painted me a picture which hangs on my refrigerator. It is purple with a splash of green and yellow. Purple was Zach's favorite color. I still brag on that picture because he did such a good job.

I also learned some incredible lessons on faith and love from Keith and Molly. Zach was loved like God had intended parents to love. There is nothing Keith and Molly would not have done for him. I am not sure I can explain it, but I never got over that. The depth of their love for him was so obvious to me I would often end up crying during most of our interviews. My crying actually became a joke between us. I am not a parent so it was hard for me to grasp loving so much and still being at complete peace knowing the end could be soon. Yet, even during those last difficult days, their faith never wavered. It is an amazing thing to witness that kind of faith in action.

Before Zach, I did not know the word "progeria." Now, I do. Zach may not have lived a long life but Zach lived life well. Keith and Molly, thank you for allowing me to tell your precious child's story. I will never forget him.

Tribute by Kate Morgan, Executive Director of Southwest Service Dogs:

My friendship with Zachary started the same way most contacts with potential clients start, with a phone call. Molly called to tell me about her youngest son, Zachary, whom she thought would benefit from a service dog. She explained his situation to me and that she had been searching for an organization which might have a dog for him.

Most service dog organizations, as a matter of policy, do not place dogs with children as young as Zachary, but Molly was insistent and seemed to be such a caring and nurturing mother that I began to feel that factors other than age should be our guideline. Molly sent me several photos of Zachary, with and without family members present. I was convinced that I at least needed to meet them.

When I walked through their front door the first thought that went through my mind was "is it even possible to train a big golden retriever to be gentle enough with a child so young and so delicate?" Zachary was so tiny and so fragile looking. I immediately was filled with concern about the dog's paws and that one gentle touch might tear his fragile skin.

At first Zachary was fearful of the dogs. After all, even a wagging tail might deliver a painful blow. However, he quickly learned that he could trust these dogs, and he would giggle happily at the many silly things the dogs would do, like bringing toys to him or giving him a lick with their scratchy tongues. Zachary's whole family was very supportive. The minute brother Derek and sister Courtney got home from school they would check up on Zachary. Zachary would stretch out his arms to Courtney and she would swing him up onto her hip and cart him through the house or play games with him. And Derek would protect him as only a big brother can.

When I drove home that night I was determined to find a dog that would work for him. Molly had impressed on me her concern about making this happen as quickly as possible. Because his progeria was so aggressive, they didn't know how long they would have Zachary. We were able to place a dog named Hobbs with Zachary soon after. Hobbs and Zachary were inseparable, with Hobbs providing companionship for Zachary through some of his most trying times, and Zachary and his family providing Hobbs with the best life any dog could imagine.

Zachary had a huge impact on Southwest Service Dogs as an organization. Despite all the family was going through, they still thought of others. They started fundraising for us by sending an email that spread all across the United States. Donations came in from all over, along with cards and letters wishing Zachary and his family well. Their thanks gave us a huge sense of accomplishment.

Zachary touched many lives, and his family very generously told his story to the world. This ripple effect continues as the Moore family continues to teach people, especially children, about the importance of appreciating the differences in all of us. People may look different on the outside, but they all have the same feelings and needs. I am extremely grateful I was allowed to share in Zachary's short life and to meet the Moore family. God bless Zachary and the Moore family.

Tribute by Captain Don Muse, Oklahoma County Sheriff's Office:

One evening I was busy doing something around the house. I don't remember what, but I was catching bits and pieces of the news on television. I caught part of a story on a little boy named Zachary Moore, who had a disease that causes early aging. I thought about what it would be like to be a parent of such a child. To know your child will die before you do. The thought depressed me and I thanked God for my children and grandchildren and went on about my business. I am a sheriff's deputy with the Oklahoma County Sheriff's Office, and the next day this child was the topic of conversation with several of the deputies I work with. I remember one guy in particular, Jason Ledford, saying that we need to do something as a group for this boy and his family. Jason and others came to me and expressed their feelings that perhaps we needed to adopt this young man into our unit. I was enthusiastic and Jason and the others came up with an idea to make young Zachary an honorary deputy. I was drafted to write a letter explaining the plan to Zachary's parents. They approved the plan and every deputy jumped on the bandwagon. A miniature uniform was made complete with patches, nametag, collar brass, and a badge. A miniature motorized car was ordered and the deputies painted it and outfitted it with lights, siren and sheriff's decals.

The day came when everything was ready and a sheriff's office caravan left Oklahoma City for Stillwater, home of our newest member, Lieutenant Zachary Moore (honorary) and his trusted K-9 sidekick, Sergeant Hobbs. A party was held and Sheriff Whetsel presented Zachary his badge. Zachary and his dad rode in a sheriff's cruiser. Zachary insisted the lights and siren be going at all times. By the end of the day there was no doubt Zachary and his family had given the deputies far more than we had given them. Our youngest deputy had won the hearts and minds of all involved.

Zachary became an inspiration to the entire sheriff's office. Make no mistake about it though, Zachary was ours. He was "assigned" by the grace of God to our department, and we loved him. Zachary and his family had an open invitation to visit us anytime. They came to our special events and unit parties. Each time they did it was a thing of love. You cannot watch Zachary without feeling a special warmth confirming there is a plan in our world and a place for each of us. Spending time with Zachary reminded us our problems were not as insurmountable as we thought. In a world full of hate, spending time with Zachary reminded us that goodness and love still exists in infinite quantities.

When the news of Zachary's death was heard at our office, people got quiet. The usual joking stopped and many of us found ourselves lost in thoughts and memories of a "child of wonder" who brought joy into the hearts of everyone fortunate enough to meet him.

A few months earlier I was struggling with a serious illness and spent days in the hospital for treatment. I was so surprised to see Zachary and his mom enter my hospital room one day for an unexpected visit. Zachary's hospital visit was a turning point for me. My spirits were lifted as Zachary shared his precious time with me in the hospital during my time of challenge.

Zachary has made an impact on all of us, and he will always be in our hearts and prayers. The sheriff's office will always display a photograph of our Lieutenant Zachary Moore to remind us of a small man who made a huge impact on us all.

Thank you, Zachary, for being who you were.

Tribute given by Zachary's preschool teacher, Jane Turner:

Molly and Keith asked me to talk about Zachary as I knew
him . . . my student at The Richmond Early Childhood Center.

Before I do that, I must thank Molly and Keith on behalf of
all the teachers, therapists and children for trusting us to be a
part of Zachary's life. When you have a medically fragile child,
it would be easier to make the decision to educate him or her at
home and not risk illness or other challenges that accompany
being present in the world. You chose to let Zachary have a life
which for him was a preschool experience that all young children need and deserve. He was not sheltered. He was not iso-
lated. He was present in the world . . . in the community, in
church and in school. How brave you were to allow this to happen. He deserved to live a full life, and you honored that.

A devoted mother and father. Watching you with Zachary
was like watching how I believe God cares for each of us . . . with
gentleness, firmness, encouragement, and often with a nudge of
encouragement to keep trying. And always close by allowing for
mistakes, forgiveness and the opportunity to try again.

My special memories of Zachary:

- When our preschool door opens, I will continue to remember the bright smile that shone in his eyes when
  he entered the classroom.
- I will remember a tilted head and downcast eyes when
  new situations arose or the attention of others was too
  much.
- I will remember the eagerness with which he approached new tasks. Gluing, painting (purple of
  course), cutting with scissors, making projects for his
  parents or a picture for his grandparents. Sometimes we
  had to coax him and show him what to do. Then one of
  us would say, "It's your turn, would you like to try?"
  Then came the familiar "uh huh." Sometimes we would

have to take the scissors away from Molly and give them back to Zachary!

- With Ms. Sheila in adaptive physical education, Zachary loved balloons, beanbags, and riding on the red scooter with his friends. Once we even hooked Hobbs to the scooter so he could pull the children. much to their delight. Thank you, Molly, for the inventive ways you found to make all the children at ease.
- I will remember the Bear Hunt Song (a song I understand all the Moore family knows by heart), Monkey and the Alligator song and puppets, Five Green and Speckled Frogs and the color song. Zachary would wear colorful clothes to school so his mom could help him stand up when each color was called.
- The color purple.
- A loving thank-you book with illustrations from the kindergarten students given to Zachary and Molly for giving a speech about progeria, differences, and service dogs to their classes.
- An OSU scarf lovingly made by Ms. Coltharp for Zachary just because she wanted to.
- Cool Whip . . . who would have thought that such a little guy could eat so much Cool Whip . . . especially when it was supposed to be an art project?
- The word "me" or "uh huh" or "macky now".
- Vanilla wafers.
- Hanging snowflakes in the classroom. I later found one on my computer screen placed there by Zachary and Molly.
- Pictures for grandparents and especially Dad.
- The love of a big brother for a little sister Heidi.
- A Golden Retriever named Hobbs.
- Elephants.
- Barney.
- The opportunity to sing "Five Green and Speckled Frogs" one last time in the hospital.
- I will remember the influence Zachary had on the school children and school personnel. When Zachary

began school, Molly, Zachary and Hobbs gave a presentation to all the Pre-K and Kindergarten students to
help them understand about Zachary and why he
needed Hobbs. The love and compassion given to
Zachary by the children I will remember all my life. Of
course their favorite part of the presentation was when
Hobbs took off Zachary's socks with his teeth.

Zachary helped a whole new group of friends learn how to
respect and care for each other, to understand about differing
abilities, to know that we all love to play, laugh, feel safe, and be
a child. When Diana Ross and I went to see Zachary at the hospital on Monday, we took banners signed by all the Pre-K and
Kindergarten children. For many of these children, Zachary was
their first friend living with challenges—what a friend.

The Building/Maintenance/Operations Department for the
school system headed by John Anders was touched by Zachary's
life. Lynn Witzen and I enlisted his help to create a chair for
Zachary. One day John, Artie Edwards, and Doug Heid came to
our room to meet Zachary, get some measurements and talk
with Lynn and Molly. Artie and Doug enlisted the help of some
businesses in town and from that came not one, but two of the
most incredible chairs created with love. My friend Artie told me
that it was the most meaningful job he has held in all the years
of working for Stillwater Public Schools. Zachary taught me that
we needed to find creative ways to make adaptations . . . even
having Zachary sit in his chair on top of the table. I have pictures!

Ms. Kari explored ways to help Zachary be mobile and engaged
in activities within the classroom. With Ms. Kari's help Zachary acquired a "cool set of wheels," a wheelchair that set him free and gave
him new independence, what every child wants and needs.

Ms. Lynn now knows more about elephants that paint than
anyone. Today all the teachers, therapists and family are launch-
ing purple balloons after the celebration of Zachary's life. One of
the balloons will have Nellie the elephant's picture on it. Zachary
painted a picture for Nellie, and Nellie painted a picture for
Zachary. Nellie lives in California!

Zachary helped his friends in his class learn to sit still for song time, because that was his favorite part of the day, not to be missed!

Ms. Cindy, Ms. Kristen and Ms. Tracy loved Zachary's spirit. Their love of young children inspired them to create calendars for our students using handprints and footprints. Now Zachary's parents have forever handprints and footprints for 2006 . . . what a gift.

The length of our journey in life isn't significant. What is significant are the lives we touch while we are here. Thank you, Zachary, for the honor of knowing you and for the way you touched so many in your life.

You are my champion.

Tribute by Jodi Foose; Zachary's special friend:

I don't remember a time when Zachary was not in my life. I feel like I have always known him—we were family right from the start. I found out about the Moore family from a friend who read a newspaper story about a boy with progeria—a rare aging disease. But this disease is not rare to me. I had lost my little sister, Amy, 20 years ago to progeria. I had closed the door and didn't want to feel that pain again. When I first found out about Zachary who only lived an hour's drive away from me, I knew I wanted to meet him and his family. But I was scared of opening up my broken heart after the loss of my little sister.

I called my mom and told her about Zach, and she said, "You need to meet him and his family; this would be wonderful for all of you." I remember reading the story about Zachary over and over again. I finally called information and asked for the phone number listing and WOW—just like that, I had the number. Little did I know how my life was about to change. Still, I didn't call. For weeks I would dial the number and hang up before it rang. One night when I got home from work, I sat down at my computer to read my e-mail. I opened an e-mail that my mom had forwarded to me from Audrey Gordon at The Progeria Research Foundation in Boston. It was an invite to Zachary Moore's birthday party in Stillwater. I sent an e-mail to them to introduce myself and told her about my family. In about 3 minutes, Molly sent a reply letting me know that they would love to meet me because they had never met anyone who had progeria in their family. I was going to a party!

When I first got to Stillwater that next weekend, I was nervous and excited at the same time. Walking into the party I could see Zachary sitting on top of a table from across the room. I took a deep breath and walked up to Molly and tapped her on the shoulder. When she turned around, we instantly knew each other and we just hugged—and I cried. See, I went there thinking I could offer them support but little did I know the gift I was about to receive. Molly picked up Zachary and introduced me, telling him that I had a sister just like him. I looked into his eyes and fell in love. I was so overwhelmed with how much I loved Zachary from the first moment we met. We played all day. I asked Molly and Keith if I could get a photo of the whole family and me. I guess that was our first family photo together.

I started driving to Stillwater every week to have a play-date with Zachary. We would read books, sing songs, watch Barney movies, play hide and seek, and just lay on the living room floor for hours giggling and sometimes eating candy; we both loved that.

In October 2005, my family opened the first chapter of The Progeria Research Foundation in California. And in November of the same year, Keith, Molly, Molly's mother Sandy, Zachary, and of course Hobbs and I went to Boston for PRF's *Night of Wonder 2005* fundraiser where I got to introduce my family to the Moore family. It was then that we became the Moore-Fooses. It is an unspoken bond; we are family.

See, Zachary gave me a gift that nobody knows about until now. Zachary gave me back the person I was before I lost my little sister. For 20 years, I kept Amy's memory in a box in my heart. There were no photos in my house because it just hurt too much, but my relationship with Zachary gave me closure. And now my house is covered with photos of Amy and Zachary. The pain we feel when someone leaves our life is in direct proportion to the joy they bring us while they are a part of our life. I am broken-hearted for the loss of Zachary. He is in God's hands, and I am the lucky one to have had two angels in my life: Zachary and Amy. I know they will always be with me and be a very big part of my life.

I want to thank Keith, Molly, Lindsay, Courtney, Derek, Heidi, and Hobbs for making me a part of their wonderful family and for giving me the gift of knowing Zachary; for opening my heart.

I was with Zachary, Keith, and Molly for the last 10 days of Zachary's life. The true commitment of love filled that hospital room and not once did anyone give up. Zachary's spirit will live on forever.

I love you with all my heart.

—Jodi

Message written by Molly, Zach's mom, read at his funeral:

When Zachary was given to us 3½ years ago, we knew he was a gift from God, as are all children. But we soon learned that he was more like an angel. We are still amazed at how many lives he has touched and new friends that we have made because of him. When the first news story was done about Zach, Keith and I knew that this was our way of touching and inspiring people's lives. If we could help even just one person see how Zach handled life's challenges and how as a family, we remained faithful to the Lord, then it was worth opening our life for everyone to see. We never dreamed that it would be over a course of fourteen months and nine news stories later, that we would receive over 200 letters and cards and many phone calls from people letting us know that Zach touched their life in a profound way. It was not uncommon for us to be approached in public by people that had seen his story or heard about him from a friend. They would get so excited to meet him in person. Zach did more of God's work in his short 3½ years than most of us hope to accomplish in a lifetime. Zach helped us and others to understand what is important in life. God, family, friends and then the rest of the stuff we have to deal with. Zach never complained about his disabilities or challenges. He was happy with the simple things in life. People get so caught up in material things—better clothes, bigger house, expensive cars, etc.—that they forget what life is really about. Our life here on earth is just a waiting room for the best vacation we will ever have. We all are terminal and should live our lives serving the Lord because, as the Bible says, "our days are numbered." When you leave here today, I challenge each of you to follow the example made by Zachary and make a commitment to have a positive impact on at least one person every day and to dedicate your life to making a difference. Zachary's work on this earth can continue through all of you. Find your true purpose in this life and you will celebrate the rewards in Heaven. Thank you for all your love and prayers, and may God bless all of you.

Tribute by Audrey Gordon; Executive Director of The Progeria Research Foundation:

Why am I not surprised that Zachary was so special, that he touched so many lives in such a profound way? Because children with progeria have something unique and captivating about them. It's that simple.

If you have ever had the privilege, like me, to meet and get to know a child with progeria and their family, you know what I'm talking about. And if you have not, then this book is the next best thing, giving you an inspiring glimpse of a family living with a disease that somehow gives them an insight into what it takes to get the most out of life—even if one of those lives is cut unfairly short.

It is a testament to Zach's upbeat personality and zest for life that his parents have chosen to donate a portion of the proceeds from the sale of this book to the Progeria Research Foundation. Although too late for Zach to benefit from the research that PRF promotes, he surely would want the quest for a cure to continue so that other children can benefit from it. Our hope is that we find the cure soon, so that all children living with progeria today will live long and healthy lives.

Sincerely,
Audrey Gordon
President, Executive Director
The Progeria Research Foundation
www.progeriaresearch.org

Following Zachary's passing, we received numerous messages from those who admired him. Here are a few:

- The stories of Zachary's accomplishments will be greatly missed. Thank you for showing me how to love a little deeper and appreciate life a little more. My thoughts and prayers are with you and your family.
- I am the lady in the power-chair you met at the grocery store and gave information to about the service dog organization. I was inspired by your stories of what Zachary and his service dog, Hobbs, were able to do together. Yet another example of how he touched lives. I am sorry for your loss but wanted to tell you another example of his legacy.
- When I first saw Zachary on the television news, he touched my heart so much I rushed to contribute to Southwest Service Dogs. I looked forward to receiving the organization's newsletters and hearing how Hobbs and Zachary were getting along. You guys were always in my prayers. I never believed in angels until Zachary. I firmly believe he was God's angel from heaven. God bless you and your family. How blessed you were to know him.
- To Molly: I worked at Wal-Mart and once you came through my register and we had a delightful conversation about Zachary and his service dog. You had such a positive attitude; I couldn't help but admire you.
- I love you so much. I will never forget all the good times playing with Zachary. Those were truly some of the best moments of my life. I continue to pray every day.
- Zachary is one of God's special angels, and He only let us keep him for short time to teach all of us some special lessons on life. I never knew him personally, but I always read everything in the news about him. All of you have fought a good battle, and I know God is embracing your entire family at this time and saying, "a job well done."

- My family's thoughts and prayers are with you and Zachary. We have followed his wonderful life, and I am proud to say his life had a profound affect on us all.
- Zachary is an inspiration to us all, and his life inspired me to never give up and always carry a smile and live life to the fullest.
- What a beautiful little boy. Thank you so much for sharing his story and life with us over the years. He was definitely a gift from God. His story helped me to understand and learn more of my faith in the Lord. May God bless all the family and all the friends of Zachary. You're forever in our hearts.
- Zachary came here for a reason ordained by God, and you may never know the full blessings his life will have on others, but know that there is one.
- We were all blessed to have had the chance to witness Zachary's courageous battle. All our lives have been enriched by him.
- He made me understand not to take life for granted. I have three children and I sometimes don't appreciate them the way I should. Your son touched my heart, and I thank you for sharing him with us.
- I remember reading about him when he first got his service dog, and I've been inspired by him ever since. Thank you for sharing his life story, and God bless everyone in his family.
- I watched Zachary on television and kept updated on him. He seemed so sweet and strong for a kid his age.
- How much your family, your story, and most of all Zachary have blessed and impressed so many others! Your faith, your humor, and your compassion are so inspiring. Thank you for sharing your angel with us, and please find comfort in the joy God has allowed you, even for such a brief period.
- As a grandmother of a boy around Zachary's age, I must share how his story and your words touched my heart.

God bless you all for your willingness to let the Son shine through you.

- I am so glad I met Zachary last summer. You have touched my life more than you know. I love you Zachary.
- Thank you for sharing such a wonderful life with us all. Zachary's courage and example remind us God is in control, and we should seek His will in our lives. All our lives were a little brighter because Zachary lived. Today heaven is a little brighter because he lives.
- I want you to know Zachary's story touched my heart in a profound way. I got caught up in life and forgot what is important. What an amazing little boy. The story and his father's words will have me in church with my family Sunday morning to rededicate our lives to the Lord. Thank you for your son and your story.

Home!

$\blacklozenge$ $\blacklozenge$ $\blacklozenge$

When we were driving in the car, Zachary would see cattle from the car window and he would always exclaim "Cow!" as he pointed the animal out to us all. He would often then insist we pull over and go see the cow up close. Now, remember, we live in Oklahoma, and there are a lot of cows! Many times I pulled over so we could see the cows. Zachary had conditioned me to know that things would be much easier on us all if we did what he said. Remember, he was the Boss. So we took the time to do what he wanted, and we never regretted stopping and obliging him. I can still hear him saying "bye" to the cows as we climbed back into our car to drive off.

Another one of Zachary's habits was his announcement when returning home as we turned our car onto the street our house was on. He would always exclaim "home!" It did not matter if it was day or night, and if he was asleep he always seemed to suddenly wake up to make his announcement right on cue. Our family continues to make this announcement when we turn onto our street. We feel obliged to carry this on for Zachary. It amazed me on our drive home from Zachary's funeral when Heidi broke the silence from inside our car and exclaimed "home!" as we made the turn onto our street. When I heard this I knew we were going to be all right. How encouraging one word can be when spoken with a pure heart. Maybe one of these days Zachary will again exclaim "home" when Jesus calls us all home for good.

It seems I'd arrived at the peak of my life when Zachary was alive. I can accept this for now I know I am on the downhill side of my life. This is evident without Zachary, not to mention the simple fact I'm approaching mid life. While the view from the top was the best, I sure am making the most of the downhill side for with it comes wisdom and opportunity.

One of the best things about Zachary was his ability to make others happy. I remember being at home with nothing much to do. Zachary made this time so much fun and memorable for me. Zachary taught me time and again how you control your own happiness. He was able to find continual happiness in spite of his constant challenges. He did this through an uncompromising desire to be happy. He created his own happiness and did not wait on others to provide, or conditions to change, or needs be fulfilled to then be happy. Zachary accomplished this through his faith. His desire for happiness was always met and in turn you could not help but be happy when with him. His desire and determination for faith and happiness is a simple quality so difficult for me to accomplish. But I will work on it every day until I am called unto heaven as Zachary was.

Zachary was indeed a special child. The thing I miss the most about him is the inspiration he gave me and many others through his faith and happiness. My family has received hundreds of letters from people letting us know how they appreciate Zachary. I will never know the number of people he was able to help in his life. However, I do know that God knows the exact number, and now Zachary's true reward is given to him. He always loved and cared so much for others with a servant's heart. In return, he received the true love of many around him. My duty to Zachary is now clear to me. May his legacy spread the good news of what love can accomplish. I hope Zachary's "roll call" in heaven is a long list of those who love him and may his story continue to inspire those seeking, needing, and wanting inspiration in their lives. Your Attitude really is YOUR Choice!

Dedication: I dedicate this book on behalf of Zachary "Boss" Moore to all his family, friends, and the children with progeria or other terminal illnesses and their families.

**Indianapolis
Marion County
Public Library**

**Renew by Phone
269-5222**

Renew on the Web
www.imcpl.org

For General Library Information
please call 269-1700